WHAT DID JESUS SAY?

WHAT DID JESUS SAY?

Truth and Grace That Fill Our Spiritual Void

Ralph E. Williams

Everything Jesus said in the four Gospels
integrated into one coherent chronological flow

RIVER BIRCH PRESS

Daphne, Alabama

What Did Jesus Say?
by Ralph E. Williams
Copyright ©2021 Ralph E. Williams
All rights reserved. This book is protected under the copyright laws of the United States of America. This book may not be copied or reprinted for commercial gain or profit.

All biblical text in this book is taken from the World English Bible (WEB), published in 2000. It is an update of the 1901 American Standard Version. I chose this translation because of its commitment to use normal modern English while keeping close to a literal "word for word" translation. It is in the public domain.

ISBN   978-1-951561-59-8   (Print)
ISBN   978-1-951561-60-4   (E-book)
For Worldwide Distribution
Printed in the U.S.A

                        River Birch Press
                          P.O. Box 868
                       Daphne, AL 36526

I dedicate this book in loving memory to my parents,

James J. Williams ("Jack")
Elizabeth W. Williams ("Betty")

They passed away many years ago
and now (I am confident) dwell with the Lord.

Acknowledgments

I acknowledge the support of my wife, Linda Lavelle Williams. She was a constant source of encouragement and continues to be so. As an RN, she has spent her life helping and serving others.

I acknowledge my brother, Carl Williams, who also has spent a considerable portion of his life in a profession focused on helping people.

I acknowledge the huge help of my agent, Keith Carroll, whose perspective and advice made this a much better book than when first submitted.

I acknowledge River Birch Press, publisher Brian Banashak, and Editor-in-Chief Kathy Banashak for their considerable help, support, and editorial expertise. Moreover, my book critically required a considerable variety of font and format for specific purposes. That created extra work for the publisher. I am especially grateful for their ability and willingness to accommodate those requirements.

But most of all, I humbly praise the Lord God of the universe for allowing me to serve Him with this book. Fortunately for me (and all of us), God often allows very imperfect people to further His purpose. I am one such person.

Table of Contents

Introduction   *ix*
Who Is Who   *xiii*
Preface   *xvii*
1. It All Begins   *1*
2. Disciples Called; Healing Begins   *12*
3. Real Meaning of the Sabbath   *21*
4. Sermon on the Mount   *26*
5. Healing and Forgiveness   *37*
6. A Series of Parables   *45*
7. Power over Nature and Death   *51*
8. Feeding Multitudes   *60*
9. Death, Resurrection, Transfiguration   *72*
10. Greatness, Offenses, Forgiveness   *78*
11. Go and Sin No More   *87*
12. The Good Samaritan; Persistence in Prayer   *102*
13. Humble Will Be Exalted   *112*
14. Straying Prodigal Son   *122*
15. I am Resurrection and Life   *128*
16. All Things are Possible; Jesus Is Anointed   *138*
17. Final Week; Triumphal Entry   *148*
18. Greatest Commandment   *157*
19. Great Tribulation Coming   *163*
20. Public Ministry Completed   *173*
21. Last Gathering; Passover   *177*
22. The Lord's Supper   *182*
23. Arrest and Trial   *196*
24. Crucifixion, Death, Burial   *206*
25. Resurrection!   *212*
26. Great Commission   *221*
Appendix
  A. Methodology   *225*
  B. Notation   *231*

Introduction

It seemed useful to me to gather together everything Jesus said as recorded in the four Gospels (Mathew, Mark, Luke, and John) of the New Testament of the Bible, plus a tiny bit from the first of the book of Acts, and integrate them into one coherent chronological flow.

Jesus' words are in **bold**. Although the intended focus is on what Jesus said and did, a considerable amount of surrounding Biblical text is included to put His words clearly into context, to relate the impact of His words, or to describe major events impacting His actions. Occasionally this results in extended passages in which He says little.

You will gain a three-fold benefit from this book:

- First, it provides a more complete compilation of what Jesus said and did than is readily apparent by reading each Gospel separately, with different events and different detail distributed among them.

- Second, it is very compelling and instructive to read Jesus' words combined in this continuous manner.

- Third, it is a useful introduction for those just beginning to explore Christianity and is an encouragement to read and study the full Bible.

This book compiles what Jesus said while on the planet as reported in the New Testament. Jesus' words are in **bold** to distinguish them from surrounding biblical text. Other than chapter titles and footnotes, all non-biblical text is in italics—mainly descriptive subheadings and some commentary.

Beneath each subheading is noted the physical location of the event(s) and biblical references to the verses assembled thereafter. If none is shown, it is a continuation of the previous indication. See the Appendix ("Notation") for more detail.

Not wanting to impede the flow of the text, I limited myself to very few footnotes or other commentary. However, those with limited biblical knowledge may find some passages unclear or confusing. If so, the Internet is a quick and easy reference source in such cases. (You usually can just type a phrase from a verse into a search engine.)

This chronological flow is divided into separate chapters for readability. I've included my own brief summary of each chapter's major content after each chapter title.

The chronological order of events is based on "Harmony of the Gospels" documents, but residual uncertainties exist (discussed in Appendix).

This compilation of what Jesus said is offered as one tool among many. I think it is a powerful tool. But it certainly does not substitute for reading and studying the full Bible.

The Bible tells us Jesus was "full of grace and truth" (John 1:14). As I read through all that Jesus says and does, these concepts appear over and over. We err when we emphasize one at the expense of the other. Both are essential. I respectfully encourage you to keep both Truth and Grace in mind as you read through what Jesus told us and how He acted.

Author John Ortberg in his book, *The Life You Always Wanted,* makes the point that for Christians "the greatest danger is not that we will renounce our faith—but that we will settle for a mediocre version of it." One can be mediocre in either Truth or Grace. I trust that taking seriously all that Jesus says will help us exceed mediocrity both in complying with His Truth and exhibiting His Grace.

Full detail on the methodology used to formulate this integrated, chronological text and discussion of four special situations are given in the Appendix ("Methodology").

Who Is Who

Almost everyone is familiar with Jesus, His earthly parents, Mary and Joseph, and the twelve disciples (as a group, if not by name). But there are other recurring people and groups that are significant in the four Gospels. Even some Christians may be a bit hazy about some of them. So here is a working summary for reference:

Gentiles:
Biblically, a Gentile was anyone who was not a Jew. So from the Jewish perspective, Gentiles were everyone else, the other peoples or nations not of their faith system. Jesus was a Jew.

[As to who is a Jew, that can become somewhat technical. In biblical times, it was relatively straightforward. A Jew was a member of the Israelite people (the descendants of Abraham through Isaac and Jacob) and their associated faith system. In modern times and in common usage, various elements of race, ethnicity, nationhood, and religion are sometimes invoked, and viewpoints vary.]

John the Baptist:
A forerunner of Jesus foretold by Isaiah (Isaiah 40:3) and Malachi (Malachi 3:1). Like Jesus, his birth and name were announced by an angel. John's mother, Elizabeth, was a relative of Mary, the mother of Jesus. John foretold the coming of the Messiah (Jesus) and baptized Jesus in the river Jordan.

Mary:
There are a number of persons named "Mary" referred to in the New Testament. The ones that appear here are:

- Mary, the mother of Jesus (often referred to today as the Virgin Mary).

- Mary Magdalene (meaning from the city of Magdala, near the coast). Jesus cast seven demons from her (we do not know her illness) and she became a follower of Jesus. She was present at his crucifixion and was one of the first witnesses of his resurrection.

  Note: In the Middle Ages, Mary Magdalene was characterized as a repentant prostitute by some, and that false attribution has survived to this day in some quarters. There is no biblical basis for this, and it should be considered false.

- Mary (of Bethany), the sister of Martha and Lazarus. This is the Mary who sat at Jesus' feet listening to his teaching while her sister, Martha, worked in the kitchen (and complained about it). She is also the Mary who anointed Jesus' feet with oil and wiped them with her hair.

- Mary, the mother of the disciple James and his brother, Joseph. (Note: there were two disciples named James.) She was present at Jesus' death and resurrection (with Mary Magdalene).

- Mary the wife of Clopas. This Mary is mentioned with this description (the wife of Clopas) only once in the New Testament, listed among the women standing near the cross. Her identity is ambiguous. For example, the word (in its context) translated as "wife" could possibly mean "daughter," "cousin," or even "sister." Making inferences from other Bible passages, some scholars suspect she might be Mary, the mother of James and Joseph, and not a "new" Mary. There are other possibilities. We just don't know.

Herod:
There are five persons referred to as "Herod" in the New Testament, all of them related. So when one reads of the death of Herod during the childhood of Jesus, then reads of the grown Jesus appearing before Herod, it can be confusing unless one knows it's not the same Herod. The two Herods that appear here are these (neither was a very nice guy!):

- Herod the Great—King of Judea (technically a Roman client king, but granted the title "King of Judea" by the Roman Senate). He is the Herod who ordered the male babies of Bethlehem killed, trying to ensure the infant Jesus did not survive.
- Herod Antipas—Son of Herod the Great, Tetrarch of Galilee and Perea. This is the Herod who put John the Baptist to death, and who sent Jesus back to Pilate.

Pontius Pilate:
The Roman procurator (or governor) of the Roman province of Judea. He is the one who issued the official order sentencing Jesus to death by crucifixion.

Scribes:
A learned group of Jews who studied the Scriptures and served as copyists, interpreters, and teachers.

Pharisees:
A Jewish political and religious party committed to strictly observing and enforcing the Law of God as interpreted by the Scribes. They also strictly supported the tradition of the elders—the man-made body of oral and written rules that had grown up over time, purporting to be applications of the Law of Moses (as given by God). The Pharisees regarded these rules almost as important as the Scripture itself. This brought them into conflict with Jesus.

Sadducees:
A Jewish faction composed largely of upper class Jews. Unlike the Pharisees, they accepted only the first five books of the Old Testament (the Pentateuch) and discounted the authority or canonical status of all the other Old Testament books. This led them to deny the resurrection of the dead. Unlike the Pharisees, they rejected the tradition of the elders.

Sanhedrin:
The highest ruling body and court of justice among the Jews—essentially a Supreme Court. It also acted as a legislative body in some respects. It was usually headed by the High Priest of Israel and had 70 other members.

Other terms for Jesus:
Jesus is sometimes referred to (either by Himself or by others) using various titles. Among them are the following:

Son of God – emphasizing His deity, His divinity
Son of Man – emphasizing His humanity (combined with His deity)
Lord – emphasizing His deity and that He rules over us
Messiah – "The anointed one" or "the chosen one."
        Old Testament term for the predicted and anticipated
        Savior of the Jews
Christ – New Testament term for the Messiah

Preface

The Old Testament of the Bible tells the story of God's creation of the universe and His interaction with humanity during the period before Jesus appeared on earth. Both Old and New Testaments contain a considerable number of prophecies, hundreds of which have already been fulfilled exactly. None have been shown false. Some are still pending.

There are around 332 prophecies in the Old Testament about the Messiah (the anticipated savior of the Jews). Jesus was the fulfillment of those prophecies. Here are a very few examples to illustrate the point:

Virgin birth: Isaiah 7:14
Triumphal entry: Zechariah 9:9
30 pieces of silver: Zechariah 11:12,13
Casting lots for His clothes: Psalm 22:18

The following is a summary of major events around and after the birth of Jesus, but before any of His words were documented in the New Testament.

The angel Gabriel appears to Mary, a virgin betrothed to Joseph, in their town of Nazareth in Galilee. He tells her she will conceive a son through the power of the Holy Spirit and that she will name him Jesus.

Joseph and Mary travel from Nazareth to Bethlehem (about 90 miles or at least a three-day trip) to be registered in the census declared by Caesar Augustus. It is here that Jesus is born.

An angel of the Lord appears to shepherds, announcing, "I bring you good news of great joy which will be to all the people. For there is born to you, this day, in the city of David *[Bethlehem]* a Savior, who is Christ the Lord" (Luke 2:8-12).

These shepherds visit Jesus in Bethlehem and relate what the Lord revealed to them.

After about 40 days, Mary and Joseph travel to Jerusalem (only five miles from Bethlehem) to present Jesus at the temple and make a sacrifice per Jewish custom. There they met a man named Simeon to whom the Holy Spirit had revealed that he would not see death until he had seen the Lord's Christ. Simeon holds Jesus, praises God, and proclaims he has now seen the Christ (Luke 2:27-32).

Wise men from the East come to worship Jesus, following a bright star. They come to Jerusalem and inquire about "He who has been born King of the Jews." Herod the King doesn't like the idea of another king and asks his priests and scribes where the Christ was to be born. Quoting the Scripture (Micah 5:2), they answer, Bethlehem. Herod sends the wise men to Bethlehem, telling them to report where they find Him.

The star reappears and goes before them until it stands over the location of Jesus. They fall down and worship Jesus and give Him gifts of gold, frankincense (a costly fragrance), and myrrh (a costly ointment). Divinely warned, the wise men return home without going back to Jerusalem and without reporting to Herod.

An angel appears to Joseph in a dream and orders him to flee to Egypt with Jesus, as Herod will seek to destroy Jesus. The family flees to Egypt.

Herod, angry that he has not found Jesus, resolves to ensure Jesus does not survive. He orders the death of all male children in Bethlehem and all its districts who are two years old or younger. This fails, of course, since Joseph, Mary, and Jesus have already fled to Egypt.

After Herod is dead, an angel again appears to Joseph in a dream and orders him to return to Israel. The family goes to Nazareth and dwells there.

─ 1 ─
It All Begins

The first words of Jesus recorded in the Gospels are when He was visiting the Temple at age twelve. He next appears in the gospels when He is baptized by John the Baptist, marking the beginning of His adult ministry. This chapter also includes the famous verse, "For God so loved the world that He gave His one and only Son, that whoever believes in Him should not perish, but have eternal life." Jesus asserts His divinity to the Samaritan women at the well and many there come to believe in Him.

Jesus at the Temple at age 12

Location: Jerusalem   Source: Lk. 2:41-52

His parents went every year to Jerusalem at the feast of the Passover. When he was twelve years old, they went up to Jerusalem according to the custom of the feast, and when they had fulfilled the days, as they were returning, the boy Jesus stayed behind in Jerusalem.

Joseph and his mother didn't know it, but supposing him to be in the company, they went a day's journey, and they looked for him among their relatives and acquaintances.

When they didn't find him, they returned to Jerusalem, looking for him. It happened after three days they found him in the temple, sitting in the midst of the teachers, both listening to them and asking them questions. All who heard him were amazed at his understanding and his answers.

When they saw him, they were astonished, and his mother said to him, "Son, why have you treated us this way? Behold, your father and I were anxiously looking for you."

He said to them, **"Why were you looking for me? Didn't you know that I must be in my Father's house?"**

They didn't understand the saying which he spoke to them.

He went down with them, and came to Nazareth. He was subject to them, and his mother kept all these sayings in her heart. Jesus advanced in wisdom and stature, and in favor with God and men.

The baptism of Jesus by John the Baptist
Location: Jordan River   *Source: Mt. 3:13-17*

Then Jesus came from Galilee to the Jordan to John, to be baptized by him. But John would have hindered him, saying, "I need to be baptized by you, and you come to me?"

But Jesus, answering, said to him, **"Allow it now, for this is the fitting way for us to fulfill all righteousness."** Then he allowed him.

Jesus, when he was baptized, went up directly from the water: and behold, the heavens were opened to him. He saw the Spirit of God descending as a dove, and coming on him. Behold, a voice out of the heavens said, "This is my beloved Son, in whom I am well pleased."

Jesus tempted by the devil
Location: Judean desert wilderness   *Source: Mt. 4:1-11*

Then Jesus was led up by the Spirit into the wilderness to be tempted by the devil. When he had fasted forty days and forty nights, he was hungry afterward. The tempter came and said to him, "If you are the

It All Begins

Son of God, command that these stones become bread."

But he answered, **"It is written, 'Man shall not live by bread alone, but by every word that proceeds out of the mouth of God.'"**

Then the devil took him into the holy city. He set him on the pinnacle of the temple, and said to him, "If you are the Son of God, throw yourself down, for it is written,

> 'He will give his angels charge concerning you.' and, 'On their hands they will bear you up, So that you don't dash your foot against a stone.'"

Jesus said to him, **"Again, it is written, 'You shall not test the Lord, your God.'"**

Again, the devil took him to an exceedingly high mountain, and showed him all the kingdoms of the world, and their glory. He said to him, "I will give you all of these things, if you will fall down and worship me."

Then Jesus said to him, **"Get behind me, Satan! For it is written, 'You shall worship the Lord your God, and him only shall you serve.'"**

Then the devil left him, and behold, angels came and ministered to him.

John the Baptist proclaims Jesus

Location: Beyond the Jordan River *Source: Jn. 1:29*

On the next day, he saw Jesus coming to him, and said, "Behold, the Lamb of God, who takes away the sin of the world!"

What Did Jesus Say?

Jesus meets future disciples Andrew and Simon Peter
Source: Jn. 1:35-42

Again, on the next day, John *[the Baptist]* was standing with two of his disciples, and he looked at Jesus as he walked, and said, "Behold, the Lamb of God!" The two disciples heard him speak, and they followed Jesus.

Jesus turned, and saw them following, and said to them, **"What are you looking for?"**

They said to him, "Rabbi" (which is to say, being interpreted, Teacher), "where are you staying?"

He said to them, **"Come, and see."**

They came and saw where he was staying, and they stayed with him that day. It was about the tenth hour *[4pm]*. One of the two who heard John, and followed him, was Andrew, Simon Peter's brother. He first found his own brother, Simon, and said to him, "We have found the Messiah!" (which is, being interpreted, Christ). He brought him to Jesus.

Jesus looked at him, and said, **"You are Simon the son of Jonah. You shall be called Cephas"** (which is by interpretation, Peter).

Jesus calls disciples Philip and Nathanael
Source: Jn. 1:43-51

On the next day, he was determined to go forth into Galilee, and he found Philip. Jesus said to him, **"Follow me."**

Now Philip was from Bethsaida, of the city of Andrew and Peter. Philip found Nathanael, and said to him, "We have found him, of whom Moses in the law, and the prophets, wrote: Jesus of Nazareth, the son of Joseph."

It All Begins

Nathanael said to him, "Can any good thing come out of Nazareth?"

Philip said to him, "Come and see."

Jesus saw Nathanael coming to him, and said about him, **"Behold, an Israelite indeed, in whom is no deceit!"**

Nathanael said to him, "How do you know me?"

Jesus answered him, **"Before Philip called you, when you were under the fig tree, I saw you."**

Nathanael answered him, "Rabbi, you are the Son of God! You are King of Israel!"

Jesus answered him, **"Because I told you, 'I saw you underneath the fig tree,' do you believe? You will see greater things than these!"** He said to him, **"Most assuredly, I tell you, hereafter you will see heaven opened, and the angels of God ascending and descending on the Son of Man."**

First miracle of Jesus reported in the Gospels—
water into wine

Location: Cana, in Galilee *Source: Jn. 2:1-11*

The third day, there was a marriage in Cana of Galilee. Jesus' mother was there. Jesus also was invited, with his disciples, to the marriage. When the wine ran out, Jesus' Mother said to him, "They have no wine."

Jesus said to her, **"Woman, what does that have to do with you and me? My hour has not yet come."**

His mother said to the servants, "Whatever he says to you, do it." Now there were six water pots of stone set there after the Jews' manner of purifying, containing two or three metretes *[20 to 30 gallons]* apiece.

Jesus said to them, **"Fill the water pots with water."** They filled them up to the brim. He said to them, **"Now draw some out, and take it to the ruler of the feast."** They took it.

When the ruler of the feast tasted the water now become wine, and didn't know where it came from (but the servants who had drawn the water knew), the ruler of the feast called the bridegroom, and said to him, "Everyone serves the good wine first, and when the guests have drunk freely, then that which is worse. You have kept the good wine until now!" This beginning of his signs Jesus did in Cana of Galilee, and revealed his glory; and his disciples believed in him.

First cleansing of the temple

Location: Jerusalem *Source: Jn. 2:13-22*

The Passover of the Jews was at hand, and Jesus went up to Jerusalem. He found in the temple those who sold oxen, sheep, and doves, and the changers of money sitting. He made a whip of cords, and threw all out of the temple, both the sheep and the oxen; and he poured out the changers' money, and overthrew their tables.

To those who sold the doves, he said, **"Take these things out of here! Don't make my Father's house a marketplace!"**

His disciples remembered that it was written, "Zeal for your house will eat me up."

The Jews therefore answered him, "What sign do you show to us, seeing that you do these things?"

Jesus answered them, **"Destroy this temple, and in three days I will raise it up."**

The Jews therefore said, "Forty-six years was this temple in building, and will you raise it up in three days?"

But he spoke of the temple of his body. When therefore he was raised from the dead, his disciples remembered that he said this, and they believed the Scripture, and the word which Jesus had said.

Teaches Nicodemus about second birth

Location: Judea *Source: Jn. 3:1-21*

Now there was a man of the Pharisees named Nicodemus, a ruler of the Jews. The same came to him by night, and said to him, "Rabbi, we know that you are a teacher come from God, for no one can do these signs that you do, unless God is with him."

Jesus answered him, **"Most assuredly, I tell you, unless one is born anew, he can't see the kingdom of God."**

Nicodemus said to him, "How can a man be born when he is old? Can he enter a second time into his mother's womb, and be born?"

Jesus answered, **"Most assuredly I tell you, unless one is born of water and the Spirit, he can't enter into the kingdom of God! That which is born of the flesh is flesh. That which is born of the Spirit is spirit. Don't marvel that I said to you, 'You must be born anew.' The wind blows where it wants to, and you hear its sound, but don't know where it comes from and where it is going. So is everyone who is born of the Spirit."**

Nicodemus answered him, "How can these things be?"

Jesus answered him, "Are you the teacher of Israel, and don't understand these things? Most assuredly I tell you, we speak that which we know, and testify of that which we have seen, and you don't receive our witness. If I told you earthly things and you don't believe, how will you believe if I tell you heavenly things? No one has ascended into heaven, but he who descended out of heaven, the Son of Man, who is in heaven. As Moses lifted up the serpent in the wilderness, even so must the Son of Man be lifted up, that whoever believes in him should not perish, but have eternal life.

"For God so loved the world, that he gave his one and only Son, that whoever believes in him should not perish, but have eternal life. For God didn't send his Son into the world to judge the world, but that the world should be saved through him. He who believes in him is not judged. He who doesn't believe has been judged already, because he has not believed in the name of the only born Son of God.

"This is the judgment, that the light has come into the world, and men loved the darkness rather than the light; for their works were evil. For everyone who does evil hates the light, and doesn't come to the light, for fear that his works would be reproved. But he who does the truth comes to the light, that his works may be revealed, that they have been done with God."

Jesus meets Samaritan woman at Jacob's well

Location: Samaria   *Source: Jn. 4:3-42*

He left Judea, and departed again into Galilee. He needed to pass through Samaria. So he came to a city of Samaria, called Sychar, near the parcel of ground that Jacob gave to his son, Joseph. Jacob's well was there. Jesus therefore, being tired from his journey, sat down by the well. It was about the sixth hour *[noon]*. A woman of Samaria came to draw water.

It All Begins

Jesus said to her, **"Give me a drink."** For his disciples had gone away into the city to buy food.

The Samaritan woman therefore said to him, "How is it that you, being a Jew, ask for a drink from me, a Samaritan woman?" (For Jews have no dealings with Samaritans.)

Jesus answered her, **"If you knew the gift of God, and who it is who says to you, 'Give me a drink,' you would have asked him, and he would have given you living water."**

The woman said to him, "Sir, you have nothing to draw with, and the well is deep. From where then have you that living water? Are you greater than our father, Jacob, who gave us the well, and drank of it himself, as did his sons, and his cattle?"

Jesus answered her, **"Everyone who drinks of this water will thirst again, but whoever drinks of the water that I will give him will never thirst; but the water that I will give him will become in him a well of water springing up to eternal life."**

The woman said to him, "Sir, give me this water, so that I don't get thirsty, neither come all the way here to draw."

Jesus said to her, **"Go, call your husband, and come here."**

The woman answered, "I have no husband."

Jesus said to her, **"You said well, 'I have no husband,' for you have had five husbands; and he whom you now have is not your husband. This you have said truly."**

The woman said to him, "Sir, I perceive that you are a prophet. Our fathers worshiped in this mountain, and you Jews say that in Jerusalem is the place where people ought to worship."

Jesus said to her, **"Woman, believe me, the hour comes, when neither in this mountain, nor in Jerusalem, will you worship the Father. You worship that which you don't know. We worship that which we know; for salvation is from the Jews. But the hour comes, and now is, when the true worshippers will worship the Father in spirit and truth, for the Father seeks such to be his worshippers. God is spirit, and those who worship him must worship in spirit and truth."**

The woman said to him, "I know that Messiah comes," (he who is called Christ). "When he has come, he will declare to us all things."

Jesus said to her, **"I who speak to you am he."**

At this, his disciples came. They marveled that he was speaking with a woman; yet no one said, "What are you looking for?" or, "Why do you speak with her?"

So the woman left her water pot, and went away into the city, and said to the people, "Come, see a man who told me everything that I did. Can this be the Christ?" They went out of the city, and were coming to him.

In the meanwhile, the disciples urged him, saying, "Rabbi, eat." But he said to them, **"I have food to eat that you don't know about."**

The disciples therefore said one to another, "Has anyone brought him something to eat?"

Jesus said to them, **"My food is to do the will of him who sent me,** and to accomplish his work. Don't you say, 'There are yet four months until the harvest?' Behold, I tell you, lift up your eyes, and look at the fields, that they are white already to harvest. He who reaps receives wages, and gathers fruit to eternal life; that both he who sows and he who reaps may rejoice together. For in this the saying is true, 'One sows, and another reaps.' I sent you to reap that for which you haven't labored. Others have labored, and you have entered into their labor."

From that city many of the Samaritans believed in him because of the word of the woman, who testified, "He told me everything that I did." So when the Samaritans came to him, they begged him to stay with them. He stayed there two days. Many more believed because of his word.

They said to the woman, "Now we believe, not because of your speaking; for we have heard for ourselves, and know that this is indeed the Christ, the Savior of the world."

— 2 —

Disciples Called; Healing Begins

In this chapter, Jesus adds to His disciples, noting He will make them "fishers for men." He begins the acts of healing that will be a major part of His ministry.

Nobleman's son healed

Location: Cana, in Galilee Source: Jn. 4:46-54

He came therefore again to Cana of Galilee, where he made the water into wine. There was a certain nobleman whose son was sick at Capernaum. When he heard that Jesus had come out of Judea into Galilee, he went to him, and begged him that he would come down and heal his son, for he was at the point of death.

Jesus therefore said to him, **"Unless you see signs and wonders, you will in no way believe."**

The nobleman said to him, "Sir, come down before my child dies."

Jesus said to him, **"Go your way. Your son lives."**

The man believed the word that Jesus spoke to him, and he went his way. As he was now going down, his servants met him and reported, saying "Your child lives!" So he inquired of them the hour when he began to get better. They said therefore to him, "Yesterday at the seventh hour *[1 pm]*, the fever left him." So the father knew that it was at

Disciples Called; Healing Begins

that hour in which Jesus said to him, "Your son lives." He believed, as did his whole house. This is again the second sign that Jesus did, having come out of Judea into Galilee.

Jesus rejected at Nazareth

Location: Nazareth *Source: Lk. 4:16-30*

He came to Nazareth, where he had been brought up. He entered, as was his custom, into the synagogue on the Sabbath day, and stood up to read. The book of the prophet Isaiah was handed to him. He opened the book, and found the place where it was written

"The Spirit of the Lord is on me,
Because he anointed me to preach good news to the poor.
He has sent me to heal the brokenhearted,
To proclaim release to the captives,
Recovering of sight to the blind,
To deliver those who are crushed,
And to proclaim the acceptable year of the Lord."

He closed the book, gave it back to the attendant, and sat down. The eyes of all in the synagogue were fastened on him. He began to tell them, **"Today, this Scripture has been fulfilled in your hearing."**

All testified about him, and wondered at the words of grace which proceeded out of his mouth, and they said, "Isn't this Joseph's son?"

He said to them, **"Doubtless you will tell me this parable, 'Physician, heal yourself! Whatever we have heard done at Capernaum, do also here in your hometown.'"**

He said, **"Most assuredly I tell you, no prophet is acceptable in his hometown. But truly I tell you, there were many widows in Israel in the days of Elijah, when the sky was shut up three years and six** months, when a great famine came over all the land. Elijah was sent to none of them, except only to Zarephath, in the land of Sidon, to a woman who was a widow. There were many lepers in Israel in the time of Elisha the prophet, yet not one of them was cleansed, except Naaman, the Syrian."

They were all filled with wrath in the synagogue, as they heard these things; and they rose up, and threw him out of the city, and led him to the brow of the hill that their city was built on, that they might throw him off the cliff. But he, passing through the midst of them, went his way.

Jesus goes to Capernaum

Location: Capernaum   *Source: Mt. 4:13-17*

Leaving Nazareth, he came and lived in Capernaum, which is by the sea, in the region of Zebulun and Naphtali, that it might be fulfilled which was spoken through Isaiah the prophet, saying,

"The land of Zebulun and the land of Naphtali,
Toward the sea, beyond the Jordan,
Galilee of the Gentiles,
The people who sat in darkness saw a great light,
To those who sat in the region and shadow of death,
To them did light spring up."

From that time, Jesus began to preach, and to say, **"Repent! For the Kingdom of Heaven is at hand."**

Jesus comes to Galilee

Location: Galilee   *Source: Mk. 1:14-15*

Now after John *[the Baptist]* was taken into custody, Jesus came into Galilee, preaching the gospel of the kingdom of God, and saying, **"The**

Disciples Called; Healing Begins

time is fulfilled, and the kingdom of God is at hand! Repent, and believe in the gospel."

Four fishermen called as disciples

Location: Sea of Galilee   *Source: Mt. 4:18-22*

Walking by the sea of Galilee, he saw two brothers: Simon, who is called Peter, and Andrew, his brother, casting a net into the sea; for they were fishermen. *[Jesus had met them before, as noted in the previous chapter.]*

He said to them, **"Come, follow me, and I will make you fishers for men."**

They immediately left their nets, and followed him.

Going on from there, he saw two other brothers, James, the son of Zebedee, and John, his brother, in the boat with Zebedee, their father, mending their nets. He called them. They immediately left the boat and their father, and followed him.

Healing on the Sabbath

Location: Capernaum   *Source: Mk. 1:21-28*

They went into Capernaum, and immediately on the Sabbath day he entered into the synagogue and taught. They were astonished at his teaching, for he taught them as having authority, and not as the scribes.

Immediately there was in their synagogue a man with an unclean spirit, and he cried out, saying, "Ha! What do we have to do with you, Jesus, you Nazarene? Have you come to destroy us? I know you who you are: the Holy One of God."

Jesus rebuked him, saying, **"Be quiet, and come out of him!"**

The unclean spirit, convulsing him and crying with a loud voice, came out of him. They were all amazed, so that they questioned among themselves, saying, "What is this? A new teaching? For with authority he commands even the unclean spirits, and they obey him." The report of him went out immediately everywhere into all the region of Galilee and its surrounding area.

[Jesus heals Peter's mother-in-law, and many others who were brought to him.]

Preaching in Galilee

Location: Galilee   Source: Mk. 1:35-38; Lk. 4:42-43; Mk. 1:39

Early in the night, he rose up and went out, and departed into a desert place, and there prayed. Simon and those who were with him followed after him; and they found him, and told him, "All are seeking you."

He said to them, **"Let's go elsewhere into the next towns, that I may preach there also, for to this end I came forth."**

When it was day, he came out and went into an uninhabited place, and the multitudes looked for him, and came to him, and held on to him, so that he wouldn't go away from them.

But he said to them, **"I must preach the good news of the kingdom of God to the other cities also. For this reason I have been sent."** He went into their synagogues throughout all Galilee, preaching and casting out demons.

Disciples Called; Healing Begins

Jesus preaches from Simon's boat;
Miraculous catch of fish

Location: Sea of Galilee *Source: Lk. 5:1-11*

Now it happened, while the multitude pressed on him and heard the word of God, that he was standing by the lake of Gennesaret *[Sea of Galilee]*. He saw two boats standing by the lake, but the fishermen had gone out of them, and were washing their nets. He entered into one of the boats, which was Simon's, and asked him to put out a little from the land. He sat down and taught the multitudes out of the boat.

When he had finished speaking, he said to Simon, **"Put out into the deep, and let down your nets for a catch."**

Simon answered him, "Master, we worked all night, and took nothing; but at your word I will let down the net." When they had done this, they caught a great multitude of fish, and their net was breaking. They beckoned to their partners in the other boat, that they should come and help them. They came, and filled both boats, so that they began to sink.

But Simon Peter, when he saw it, fell down at Jesus' knees, saying, "Depart from me, for I am a sinful man, Lord." For he was amazed, and all who were with him, at the catch of fish which they had caught; and so also were James and John, sons of Zebedee, who were partners with Simon.

Jesus said to Simon, **"Don't be afraid. From now on you will catch men alive."**

When they had brought their boats to land, they left everything, and followed him.

Leper healed

Location: GalileeSource: Mk. 1:40-45

There came to him a leper, begging him, kneeling down to him, and saying to him, "If you want to, you can make me clean."

Being moved with compassion, he stretched forth his hand, and touched him, and said to him, **"I want to. Be made clean."**

When he had said this, immediately the leprosy departed from him, and he was made clean. He strictly charged him, and immediately sent him out, and said to him, **"See you say nothing to anybody, but go show yourself to the priest, and offer for your cleansing the things which Moses commanded, for a testimony to them."**

But he went out, and began to proclaim it much, and to spread about the matter, so that Jesus could no more openly enter into a city, but was outside in desert places: and they came to him from everywhere.

Paralytic forgiven and healed

Location: CapernaumSource: Mk. 2:1-12

When he entered again into Capernaum after some days, it was heard that he was in the house. Immediately many were gathered together, so that there was no more room, not even around the door; and he spoke the word to them.

Four people came, carrying a paralytic to him. When they could not come near to him for the crowd, they removed the roof where he was. When they had broken it up, they let down the mat that the paralytic was lying on.

Jesus, seeing their faith, said to the paralytic, **"Son, your sins are forgiven you."**

Disciples Called; Healing Begins

But there were some of the scribes sitting there, and reasoning in their hearts, "Why does this man speak blasphemies like that? Who can forgive sins but God alone?"

Immediately Jesus, perceiving in his spirit that they so reasoned within themselves, said to them, **"Why do you reason these things in your hearts? Which is easier, to tell the paralytic, 'Your sins are forgiven;' or to say, 'Arise, and take up your bed, and walk?' But that you may know that the Son of Man has authority on earth to forgive sins"**—he said to the paralytic—**"I tell you, arise, take up your mat, and go to your house."**

He arose, and immediately took up the mat, and went out in front of them all; so that they were all amazed, and glorified God, saying, "We never saw anything like this!"

Disciple Matthew called

Location: Capernaum   *Source: Mt. 9:9-13*

As Jesus passed by from there, he saw a man called Matthew, sitting at the tax collection office. He said to him, **"Follow me."** He got up and followed him.

It happened, as he sat at the table in the house *[Matthew's house]*, behold, many tax collectors and sinners came and sat down with Jesus and his disciples. When the Pharisees saw it, they said to his disciples, "Why does your teacher eat with the tax collectors and sinners?"

When Jesus heard it, he said to them, **"Those who are healthy have no need for a physician, but those who are sick do. But you go and learn what this means: 'I desire mercy, and not sacrifice,' for I came not to call the righteous, but sinners to repentance."**

Comments on fasting

Location: Capernaum   Source: Mk. 2:18-20; Lk. 5:36; Mk. 2:21; Lk. 5:37-39

John's disciples and the Pharisees were fasting, and they came and asked him, "Why do John's disciples and the disciples of the Pharisees fast, but your disciples don't fast?"

Jesus said to them, "**Can the sons of the bride chamber fast while the bridegroom is with them? As long as they have the bridegroom with them, they can't fast. But the days will come when the bridegroom will be taken away from them, and then will they fast in that day.**"

He also told a parable to them. "**No one puts a piece from a new garment on an old garment, or else he will tear the new, and also the piece from the new will not match the old. No one sews a piece of unshrunk cloth on an old garment, or else the patch shrinks and the new tears away from the old, and a worse hole is made.**

"**No one puts new wine into old wineskins, or else the new wine will burst the skins, and it will be spilled, and the skins will be destroyed. But new wine must be put into fresh wineskins, and both are preserved. No man having drunk old wine immediately desires new, for he says, 'The old is better.'**"

— 3 —

Real Meaning of the Sabbath

God ordained the Sabbath to be a day of rest. But the Jewish authorities in this period had created a huge legalism about "rest" with a massive number of restrictions. By His acts and words, Jesus taught they were missing the point.

Lame man healed; teaches in Jerusalem

Location: JerusalemSource: Jn. 5:1-47

After these things, there was a feast of the Jews, and Jesus went up to Jerusalem. Now in Jerusalem by the sheep gate, there is a pool, which is called in Hebrew, "Bethesda," having five porches. In these lay a great multitude of those who were sick, blind, lame, or paralyzed, waiting for the moving of the water; for an angel of the Lord went down at certain times into the pool, and stirred up the water. Whoever stepped in first after the stirring of the water was made whole of whatever disease he was afflicted with. A certain man was there, who had been sick for thirty-eight years.

When Jesus saw him lying there, and knew that he had been sick for a long time, he asked him, **"Do you want to be made well?"**

The sick man answered him, "Sir, I have no one to put me into the pool when the water is stirred up, but while I'm coming, another steps down before me."

Jesus said to him, **"Arise, take up your mat, and walk."**

Immediately, the man was made well, and took up his mat and walked. Now it was the Sabbath on that day. So the Jews said to him who was cured, "It is the Sabbath. It is not lawful for you to carry the mat." He answered them, "He who made me well, the same said to me, 'Take up your mat, and walk.'"

Then they asked him, "Who is the man who said to you, 'Take up your mat, and walk'?" But he who was healed didn't know who it was, for Jesus had withdrawn, a crowd being in the place.

Afterward Jesus found him in the temple, and said to him, **"Behold, you are made well. Sin no more, so that nothing worse happens to you."**

The man went away, and told the Jews that it was Jesus who had made him well. For this cause the Jews persecuted Jesus, and sought to kill him, because he did these things on the Sabbath.[1]

But Jesus answered them, **"My Father is still working, so I am working, too."**

For this cause therefore the Jews sought the more to kill him, because he not only broke the Sabbath, but also called God his own Father, making himself equal with God.

Jesus therefore answered them, **"Most assuredly, I tell you, the Son can do nothing of himself, but what he sees the Father doing. For whatever things he does, these the Son also does likewise. For the**

---

[1] Healing on the Sabbath was considered prohibited under Jewish law. This was one of many cases where the Jews had taken a general commandment (rest on the Sabbath) and interpreted it into a huge number of detailed laws about what could not be done. Even in Israel today, there exist "Shabbat elevators" in some buildings that automatically stop on each floor (on the Sabbath) so that one does not have to do the "work" of pushing the button.

Father loves the Son, and shows him all things that he himself does. He will show him greater works than these, that you may marvel. For as the Father raises the dead and gives them life, even so the Son also gives life to whom he desires. For neither does the Father judge any man, but he has given all judgment to the Son, that all may honor the Son, even as they honor the Father. He who doesn't honor the Son doesn't honor the Father who sent him.

"Most assuredly I tell you, he who hears my word, and believes him who sent me, has eternal life, and doesn't come into judgment, but has passed out of death into life. Most assuredly, I tell you, the hour comes, and now is, when the dead will hear the Son of God's voice; and those who hear will live. For as the Father has life in himself, even so he gave to the Son also to have life in himself. He also gave him authority to execute judgment, because he is a son of man.

"Don't marvel at this, for the hour comes, in which all that are in the tombs will hear his voice, and will come forth; those who have done good, to the resurrection of life; and those who have done evil, to the resurrection of judgment. I can of myself do nothing. As I hear, I judge, and my judgment is righteous; because I don't seek my own will, but the will of my Father who sent me.

"If I testify about myself, my witness is not valid. It is another who testifies about me. I know that the testimony which he testifies about me is true. You have sent to John, and he has testified to the truth. But the testimony which I receive is not from man. However, I say these things that you may be saved. He was the lamp that burns and shines, and you were willing to rejoice for a while in his light.

"But the testimony which I have is greater than that of John, for the works which the Father has given me to accomplish, the very works that I do, testify about me, that the Father has sent me. The

Father himself, who sent me, has testified about me. You have neither heard his voice at any time, nor seen his form. You don't have his word living in you; for whom he sent, him you don't believe.

"You search the Scriptures, because you think that in them you have eternal life; and these are they which testify about me. Yet you will not come to me, that you may have life. I don't receive glory from men. But I know you, that you don't have God's love in yourselves. I have come in my Father's name, and you don't receive me. If another comes in his own name, you will receive him.

"How can you believe, who receive glory from one another, and you don't seek the glory that comes from the only God? Don't think that I will accuse you to the Father. There is one who accuses you, even Moses, on whom you have set your hope. For if you believed Moses, you would believe me; for he wrote about me. But if you don't believe his writings, how will you believe my words?"

About the Sabbath

Location: En route to Galilee *Source: Mt. 12:1-7; Mk. 2:27-28*

At that time, Jesus went on the Sabbath day through the grain fields. His disciples were hungry and began to pluck heads of grain and to eat. But the Pharisees, when they saw it, said to him, "Behold, your disciples do what is not lawful to do on the Sabbath."

But he said to them, **"Haven't you read what David did, when he was hungry, and those who were with him; how he entered into the house of God, and ate the show bread, which was not lawful for him to eat, neither for those who were with him, but only for the priests?**

"Or have you not read in the law, that on the Sabbath day, the priests in the temple profane the Sabbath, and are guiltless? But I tell you that one greater than the temple is here. But if you had

Real Meaning of the Sabbath

known what this means, 'I desire mercy, and not sacrifice,' you would not have condemned the guiltless."

He said to them, "The Sabbath was made for man, not man for the Sabbath. Therefore the Son of Man is Lord even of the Sabbath."

Heals hand on Sabbath

Location: Galilee *Source: Mt. 12:9-12; Mk. 3:3-6*

He departed there, and went into their synagogue. And behold there was a man with a withered hand. They asked him, "Is it lawful to heal on the Sabbath day?" that they might accuse him.

He said to them, "**What man is there among you, who has one sheep, and if this one falls into a pit on the Sabbath day, will he not grab on to it, and lift it out? How much, then, is a man of more value than a sheep! Therefore it is lawful to do good on the Sabbath day.**"

He said to the man who had his hand withered, "**Stand up.**" He said to them, "**Is it lawful on the Sabbath day to do good, or to do harm? To save a life, or to kill?**"

But they were silent. When he had looked around at them with anger, being grieved at the hardening of their hearts, he said to the man, "**Stretch out your hand.**"

He stretched it out, and his hand was restored as healthy as the other. The Pharisees went out, and immediately took counsel with the Herodians[2] against him, how they might destroy him.

[Jesus formally chooses his twelve disciples after a night of prayer]

---

[2] The Herodians were a party dedicated to Herod and rule of Rome.

— 4 —

Sermon on the Mount

The "sermon on the mount" comprises this entire chapter. It is the longest continuous oration of Jesus given in the New Testament. It emphasizes His moral teachings and includes many of His best-known teachings, including the Lord's Prayer and the Golden Rule. He emphasizes obeying the spirit of the Law, not just the letter of the Law.

Location: Near Capernaum   Source: Mt. 5:1-12 (+Lk. 6:21)

Seeing the multitudes, he went up onto a mountain. When he had sat down, his disciples came to him. He opened his mouth and taught them, saying,

The Beatitudes
"Blessed are the poor in spirit, for theirs is the Kingdom of Heaven.
Blessed are those who mourn, for they shall be comforted.
Blessed are the humble, for they shall inherit the earth.
Blessed are those who hunger and thirst after righteousness, for they shall be filled.
Blessed are you who weep now, for you will laugh.
Blessed are the merciful, for they shall obtain mercy.
Blessed are the pure in heart, for they shall see God.
Blessed are the peacemakers, for they shall be called sons of God.
Blessed are those who have been persecuted for righteousness' sake, for theirs is the Kingdom of Heaven.

"Blessed are you when people reproach you, persecute you, and say all kinds of evil against you falsely, for my sake. Rejoice, and be exceedingly glad, for great is your reward in heaven. For that is how they persecuted the prophets who were before you.

The Woes
Source: Lk. 6:24-26

"But woe to you who are rich! For you have received your consolation.
Woe to you, you who are full now! For you will be hungry.
Woe to you, you who laugh now! For you will mourn and weep.
Woe, when men will speak well of you! For their fathers did the same thing to the false prophets.

Believers are salt of the earth, the light of the world
Source: Mt. 5:13-42

"You are the salt of the earth, but if the salt has lost its flavor, what will it be salted with? It is then good for nothing, but to be cast out and trodden under the feet of men. You are the light of the world. A city set on a hill can't be hid. Neither do you light a lamp, and put it under a bushel basket, but on a stand; and it shines to all who are in the house. Even so, let your light shine before men; that they may see your good works, and glorify your Father who is in heaven.

Christ fulfills the Law

"Don't think that I came to destroy the law or the prophets. I didn't come to destroy, but to fulfill. For most assuredly, I tell you, until heaven and earth pass away, not even one smallest letter or one tiny pen stroke shall in any way pass away from the law, until all things are accomplished.

"Whoever, therefore, shall break one of these least commandments, and teach others to do so, shall be called least in the Kingdom of Heaven; but whoever shall do and teach them shall be called great in the Kingdom of Heaven. For I tell you, that unless your righteousness exceeds that of the scribes and Pharisees, there is no way you shall enter into the Kingdom of Heaven.

Murder begins in the Heart

"You have heard that it was said to them of old time, 'You shall not murder;' and 'Whoever shall murder shall be in danger of the judgment.' But I tell you, that everyone who is angry with his brother without a cause shall be in danger of the judgment.

"And whoever shall say to his brother, 'Raca,' *[worthless, empty]* shall be in danger of the council; and whoever shall say, 'You fool,' shall be in danger of the fire of Gehenna *[Hell]*. If therefore you are offering your gift at the altar, and there remember that your brother has anything against you, leave your gift there before the altar, and go your way. First be reconciled to your brother, and then come and offer your gift.

"Agree with your adversary quickly, while you are with him in the way; lest perhaps the prosecutor deliver you to the judge, and the judge deliver you to the officer, and you be cast into prison. Most assuredly I tell you, you shall by no means get out of there, until you have paid the last penny.

Adultery in the heart

"You have heard that it was said, 'You shall not commit adultery;' but I tell you that everyone who gazes at a woman to lust after her has committed adultery with her already in his heart.

"If your right eye causes you to stumble, pluck it out and cast it from you. For it is profitable for you that one of your members should perish, than for your whole body to be cast into Gehenna *[Hell]*. If your right hand causes you to stumble, cut it off, and cast it from you: for it is profitable for you that one of your members should perish, and not your whole body be cast into Gehenna.

Marriage is sacred and binding
"It was also said, 'Whoever shall put away his wife, let him give her a writing of divorce,' but I tell you that whoever who puts away his wife, except for the cause of sexual immorality, makes her an adulteress; and whoever shall marry her when she is put away commits adultery.

Jesus forbids oaths
"Again you have heard that it was said to them of old time, 'You shall not make false vows, but shall perform to the Lord your vows,' but I tell you, don't swear at all: neither by heaven, for it is the throne of God; nor by the earth, for it is the footstool of his feet; nor by Jerusalem, for it is the city of the great King. Neither shall you swear by your head, for you can't make one hair white or black. But let your speech be, 'Yes, yes; No, no.' Whatever is more than these is of the evil one.

Go the second mile
"You have heard that it was said, 'An eye for an eye, and a tooth for a tooth.' But I tell you, don't resist him who is evil; but whoever strikes you on your right cheek, turn to him the other also. If any man would go to law with you and take away your coat, let him have your cloak also. Whoever compels you to go one mile, go with him two. Give to him who asks you, and don't turn away him who desires to borrow from you.

Love your enemies

Source: Mt. 5:43-45; Lk. 6:32-34; Mt. 5:47; Lk. 6:35-36; Mt. 5:48

"You have heard that it was said, 'You shall love your neighbor, and hate your enemy.' But I tell you, love your enemies, bless those who curse you, do good to those who hate you, and pray for those who spitefully use you and persecute you, that you may be sons of your Father who is in heaven. For he makes his sun to rise on the evil and the good, and sends rain on the just and the unjust.

"If you love those who love you, what credit is that to you? For even sinners love those who love them. If you do good to those who do good to you, what credit is that to you? For even sinners do the same. If you lend to those from whom you hope to receive, what credit is that to you? Even sinners lend to sinners, to receive back as much. If you only greet your friends, what more do you do than others? Don't even the tax collectors do the same?

"But love your enemies, and do good, and lend, expecting nothing back; and your reward will be great, and you will be sons of the Most High; for he is kind toward the unthankful and evil. Therefore be merciful, even as your Father is also merciful. Therefore you shall be perfect, just as your Father in heaven is perfect.

Do good to please God

Source: Mt. 6:1-34

"Be careful that you don't do your charitable giving before men, to be seen by them, or else you have no reward with your Father who is in heaven. Therefore when you do merciful deeds, don't sound a trumpet before you, as the hypocrites do in the synagogues and in the streets, that they may get glory from men. Most assuredly, I tell you, they have received their reward.

"But when you do merciful deeds, don't let your left hand know what your right hand does, so that your merciful deeds may be in secret, then your Father who sees in secret will reward you openly.

The Lord's Prayer

"When you pray, you shall not be as the hypocrites, for they love to stand and pray in the synagogues and in the corners of the streets, that they may be seen by men. Most assuredly, I tell you, they have received their reward.

"But you, when you pray, enter into your inner chamber, and having shut your door, pray to your Father who is in secret, and your Father who sees in secret will reward you openly.

"In praying, don't use vain repetitions, as the Gentiles do; for they think that they will be heard for their much speaking. Therefore don't be like them, for your Father knows what things you need, before you ask him. Pray like this.

'Our Father, who is in heaven, may your name be kept holy.
May your kingdom come.
May your will be done, as in heaven, so on earth.
Give us this day our daily bread.
Forgive us our debts, as we also forgive our debtors.
Bring us not into temptation, but deliver us from evil.
For yours is the kingdom, the power and the glory forever. Amen.'

"For if you forgive men their trespasses, your heavenly Father will also forgive you.
But if you don't forgive men their trespasses, neither will your Father forgive your trespasses.

Fasting to be seen only by God
"Moreover when you fast, don't be, as the hypocrites, with sad faces. For they disfigure their faces, that they may be seen by men to be fasting. Most assuredly I tell you, they have received their reward. But you, when you fast, anoint your head, and wash your face; that you are not seen by men to be fasting, but by your Father who is in secret, and your Father, who sees in secret, will reward you.

Lay up treasures in heaven
"Don't lay up treasures for yourselves on the earth, where moth and rust consume, and where thieves break through and steal; but lay up for yourselves treasures in heaven, where neither moth nor rust consume, and where thieves don't break through and steal; for where your treasure is, your heart will be there also.

The lamp of the body
"The lamp of the body is the eye: if therefore your eye is sound, your whole body will be full of light. But if your eye is evil, your whole body will be full of darkness. If therefore the light that is in you is darkness, how great is the darkness!

You cannot serve both God and riches
"No one can serve two masters, for either he will hate the one, and love the other; or else he will hold to one, and despise the other. You can't serve both God and Mammon *[riches or avarice]*.

Do not worry
"Therefore, I tell you, don't be anxious for your life, what you will eat, or what you will drink; nor yet for your body, what you will put on. Isn't life more than food, and the body more than clothing?

"See the birds of the sky, that they don't sow, neither do they reap, nor gather into barns. Your heavenly Father feeds them. Aren't you of much more value than they? Which of you, by being anxious, can add one cubit to the measure of his life?

"Why are you anxious about clothing? Consider the lilies of the field, how they grow. They don't toil, neither do they spin, yet I tell you that even Solomon in all his glory was not dressed like one of these. But if God so clothes the grass of the field, which today exists, and tomorrow is cast into the oven, won't he much more clothe you, you of little faith?

"Therefore don't be anxious, saying, 'What will we eat?', 'What will we drink?' or, 'With what will we be clothed?' For the Gentiles seek after all these things, for your heavenly Father knows that you need all these things. But seek first God's Kingdom, and his righteousness; and all these things will be added to you. Therefore don't be anxious for tomorrow, for tomorrow will be anxious for itself. Each day's own evil is sufficient.

Do not judge
Source: Lk. 6:37-42 (+Mt. 7:2); Mt. 7:6

"Don't judge, and you will not be judged. For with whatever judgment you judge, you will be judged. Don't condemn, and you will not be condemned. Set free, and you will be set free. Give, and it will be given to you, good measure, pressed down, shaken together, and running over, will they give into your bosom. For with the same measure you measure it will be measured back to you."

He spoke a parable to them. "Can the blind guide the blind? Won't they both fall into a pit? A disciple is not above his teacher, but everyone when he is fully trained will be like his teacher. Why do you see the speck of chaff that is in your brother's eye, but don't consider the beam that is in your own eye? Or how can you tell your brother, 'Brother, let me remove the speck of chaff that is in your eye,' when you yourself don't see the beam that is in your own eye?

"You hypocrite! First remove the beam from your own eye, and then you can see clearly to remove the speck of chaff that is in your brother's eye. Don't give that which is holy to the dogs, neither cast your pearls before the pigs, lest perhaps they trample them under their feet, and turn and tear you to pieces.

Keep asking, seeking, knocking

Source: Mt. 7:7-11

"Ask, and it will be given you. Seek, and you will find. Knock, and it will be opened to you. For everyone who asks receives. He who seeks finds. To him who knocks it will be opened. Or what man is there of you, who, if his son asks him for bread, will give him a stone? Or if he asks for a fish, who will give him a serpent? If you then, being evil, know how to give good gifts to your children, how much more will your Father who is in heaven give good things to those who ask him!

The Golden Rule

Source: Mt. 7:12

"Therefore whatever you desire for men to do to you, you shall also do to them; for this is the law and the prophets.

The narrow way; a tree and its fruit

Source: Mt. 7:13-20 (+Lk. 6:44); Lk. 6:45

"Enter in by the narrow gate; for wide is the gate, and broad is the way, that leads to destruction, and many are those who enter in by it. How narrow is the gate, and restricted is the way that leads to life! Few are those who find it.

"Beware of false prophets, who come to you in sheep's clothing, but inwardly are ravening wolves. By their fruits you will know them. For each tree is known by its own fruit. Do you gather grapes from thorns, or figs from thistles? Even so, every good tree brings forth good fruit; but the corrupt tree brings forth evil fruit. A good tree can't bring forth evil fruit, neither can a corrupt tree bring forth good fruit. Every tree that doesn't grow good fruit is cut down, and thrown into the fire. Therefore, by their fruits you will know them.

"The good man out of the good treasure of his heart brings forth that which is good, and the evil man out of the evil treasure of his heart brings forth that which is evil, for out of the abundance of the heart, his mouth speaks.

I never knew you
Source: Mt. 7:21-23

"Not everyone who says to me, 'Lord, Lord,' will enter into the Kingdom of Heaven; but he who does the will of my Father who is in heaven. Many will tell me in that day, 'Lord, Lord, didn't we prophesy by your name, by your name cast out demons, and by your name do many mighty works?' Then I will tell them, 'I never knew you. Depart from me, you who work iniquity.'

Build on the rock
Source: Mt. 7:24; Lk. 6:48; Mt. 7:25-29

"Everyone therefore who hears these words of mine, and does them, I will liken him to a wise man, who built his house on a rock. He is like a man building a house, who dug and went deep, and laid a foundation on the rock. The rain came down, the floods came, and the winds blew, and beat on that house; and it didn't fall, for it was founded on the rock.

"Everyone who hears these words of mine, and doesn't do them will be like a foolish man, who built his house on the sand. The rain came down, the floods came, and the winds blew, and beat on that house; and it fell—and great was its fall."

It happened, when Jesus had finished saying these things, that the multitudes were astonished at his teaching, for he taught them with authority, and not like the scribes.

— 5 —

Healing and Forgiveness

Acts of healing and forgiveness of sins characterized much of Jesus' ministry. These continue in this chapter. He explicitly rebukes those who sin without remorse and emphasizes the peace and rest available through Him.

Centurion's servant healed

Location: Capernaum   *Source: Mt. 8:5-13*

When he came into Capernaum, a centurion came to him, asking him, and saying, "Lord, my servant lies in the house paralyzed, grievously tormented."

Jesus said to him, **"I will come and heal him."**

The centurion answered, "Lord, I'm not worthy for you to come under my roof. Just say the word, and my servant will be healed. For I am also a man under authority, having under myself soldiers. I tell this one, 'Go,' and he goes; and to another, 'Come,' and he comes; and to my servant, 'Do this,' and he does it."

When Jesus heard it, he marveled, and said to those who followed, **"Most assuredly I tell you, I haven't found so great a faith, not even in Israel. I tell you that many will come from the east and the west, and will sit down with Abraham, and Isaac, and Jacob, in the Kingdom of Heaven, but the sons of the kingdom will be thrown** out into the outer darkness. There will be weeping and the gnashing of teeth."

Jesus said to the centurion, **"Go your way. Let it be done for you as you have believed."**

His servant was healed in that hour.

Raises widow's son from dead
Location: Nain   *Source: Lk. 7:11-17*

It happened soon afterwards, that he went to a city called Nain. Many of his disciples went with him, along with a great multitude. Now when he drew near to the gate of the city, behold, one who was dead was carried out, the only son of his mother, and she was a widow. Many people of the city were with her.

When the Lord saw her, he had compassion on her, and said to her, **"Don't cry."**

He came near and touched the coffin, and the bearers stood still. He said, **"Young man, I tell you, arise!"**

He who was dead sat up, and began to speak. He gave him to his mother. Fear took hold on all, and they glorified God, saying, "A great prophet has arisen among us!" and, "God has visited his people!" This report went out concerning him in the whole of Judea, and in all the surrounding region.

Jesus speaks of John the Baptist
Location: Galilee   *Source: Mt. 11:2-15; Lk. 7:31-35; Mt. 11:20-30*

Now when John *[the Baptist]* heard in the prison the works of Christ,

Healing and Forgiveness

he sent two of his disciples and said to him, "Are you he who comes, or should we look for another?"

Jesus answered them, **"Go and tell John the things which you hear and see: the blind receive their sight, the lame walk, the lepers are cleansed, the deaf hear, the dead are raised up, and the poor have good news preached to them. Blessed is he, whoever finds no occasion for stumbling in me."**

As these went their way, Jesus began to say to the multitudes concerning John, **"What did you go out into the wilderness to see? A reed shaken with the wind? But what did you go out to see? A man in soft clothing? Behold, those who wear soft clothing are in king's houses. But why did you go out? To see a prophet? Yes, I tell you, and much more than a prophet. For this is he, of whom it is written,**

> **'Behold, I send my messenger before your face,
> who will prepare your way before you.'**

"Most assuredly I tell you, among those who are born of women there has not arisen anyone greater than John the Baptizer; yet he who is least in the Kingdom of Heaven is greater than he. From the days of John the Baptizer until now, the Kingdom of Heaven suffers violence, and the violent take it by force. For all the prophets and the law prophesied until John. If you are willing to receive it, this is Elijah, who is to come. He who has ears to hear, let him hear."

The Lord said, **"To what then will I liken the men of this generation? What are they like? They are like children who sit in the marketplace, and call one to another, saying,**

'We piped to you, and you didn't dance.
We mourned, and you didn't weep.'

"For John the Baptizer came neither eating bread nor drinking wine, and you say, 'He has a demon.' The Son of Man has come eating and drinking, and you say, 'Behold, a gluttonous man, and a drunkard; a friend of tax collectors and sinners!' Wisdom is justified by all her children."

Woes to the impenitent cities

Then he began to denounce the cities in which most of his mighty works were done, because they didn't repent. **"Woe to you, Chorazin! Woe to you, Bethsaida!** For if the mighty works had been done in Tyre and Sidon which were done in you, they would have repented long ago in sackcloth and ashes. But I tell you, it will be more tolerable for Tyre and Sidon in the day of judgment than for you. You, Capernaum, who are exalted to Heaven, you will go down to Hades. For if the mighty works had been done in Sodom which were done in you, it would have remained until this day. But I tell you that it will be more tolerable for the land of Sodom, in the day of judgment, than for you."

Jesus gives true rest

At that time, Jesus answered, "I thank you, Father, Lord of heaven and earth, that you hid these things from the wise and understanding, and revealed them to infants. Yes, Father, for so it was well-pleasing in your sight. All things have been delivered to me by my Father. No one knows the Son, except the Father; neither does anyone know the Father, except the Son, and he to whoever the Son wants to reveal him.

"Come to me, all you who labor and are heavily burdened, and I will give you rest. Take my yoke on you, and learn from me, for I

Healing and Forgiveness

am humble and lowly in heart; and you will find rest for your souls. For my yoke is easy, and my burden is light."

Jesus' feet anointed; He forgives a sinful woman
Location: Capernaum   *Source:* Lk. 7:36-50

One of the Pharisees invited him to eat with him. He entered into the Pharisee's house, and sat at the table. Behold, a woman in the city who was a sinner, when she knew that he was reclining in the Pharisee's house, she brought an alabaster jar of ointment. Standing behind at his feet weeping, she began to wet his feet with her tears, and she wiped them with the hair of her head, kissed his feet, and anointed them with the ointment.

Now when the Pharisee who had invited him saw it, he said to himself, "This man, if he were a prophet, would have perceived who and what kind of woman this is who touches him, that she is a sinner."

Jesus answered him, **"Simon, I have something to tell you."**

He said, "Teacher, say on."

"A certain lender had two debtors. The one owed five hundred denarii, and the other fifty. When they couldn't pay, he forgave them both. Which of them therefore will love him most?"

Simon answered, "He, I suppose, to whom he forgave the most."

He said to him, **"You have judged correctly."**

Turning to the woman, he said to Simon, **"Do you see this woman? I entered into your house, and you gave me no water for my feet, but she has wet my feet with her tears, and wiped them with the hair of her head. You gave me no kiss, but she, since the time I came in,** has not ceased to kiss my feet. You didn't anoint my head with oil, but she has anointed my feet with ointment. Therefore I tell you, her sins, which are many, are forgiven, for she loved much. But to whom little is forgiven, the same loves little."

He said to her, **"Your sins are forgiven."**

Those who sat at the table with him began to say to themselves, "Who is this who even forgives sins?"

He said to the woman, **"Your faith has saved you. Go in peace."**

Bringing good news

Source: Lk. 8:1

It happened soon afterwards, that he went about through cities and villages, preaching and bringing the good news of the kingdom of God, and with him the twelve,

A house divided cannot stand

Location: Capernaum Source: Mt. 12:22-30

Then there was brought to him one possessed by a demon, blind and mute, and he healed him, so that the blind and mute man both spoke and saw. All the multitudes were amazed, and said, "Can this be the son of David?" But when the Pharisees heard it, they said, "This man does not cast out demons, except by Beelzebul, the prince of the demons."

Knowing their thoughts, Jesus said to them, **"Every kingdom divided against itself is brought to desolation, and every city or house divided against itself will not stand. If Satan casts out Satan, he is divided against himself. How then will his kingdom stand? If I by Beelzebul cast out demons, by whom do your sons cast them out? Therefore they will be your judges.**

"But if I by the Spirit of God cast out demons, then the kingdom of God has come on you. Or how can one enter into the house of the strong man, and plunder his goods, except he first bind the strong man? Then he will plunder his house. He who is not with me is against me, and he who doesn't gather with me, scatters.

The unpardonable sin
Source: Mt. 12:31-37

"Therefore I tell you, every sin and blasphemy will be forgiven men, but the blasphemy against the Spirit will not be forgiven men. Whoever speaks a word against the Son of Man, it will be forgiven him; but whoever speaks against the Holy Spirit, it will not be forgiven him, neither in this world, nor in that which is to come.

A tree is known by its fruit

"Either make the tree good, and its fruit good, or make the tree corrupt, and its fruit corrupt; for the tree is known by its fruit. You offspring of vipers, how can you, being evil, speak good things? For out of the abundance of the heart, the mouth speaks. The good man out of his good treasure brings forth good things, and the evil man out of his evil treasure brings forth evil things. I tell you that every idle word that men speak, they will give account of it in the day of judgment. For by your words you will be justified, and by your words you will be condemned."

Request for a sign; the sign of Jonah
Source: Mt. 12:38-45

Then certain of the scribes and Pharisees answered, saying, "Teacher, we want to see a sign from you."

But he answered them, "An evil and adulterous generation seeks after a sign, and there will no sign be given it but the sign of Jonah, the prophet. For as Jonah was three days and three nights in the belly of the whale, so will the Son of Man be three days and three nights in the heart of the earth.

"The men of Nineveh will stand up in the judgment with this generation, and will condemn it, for they repented at the preaching of Jonah; and behold, someone greater than Jonah is here. The queen of the south will rise up in the judgment with this generation, and will condemn it, for she came from the ends of the earth to hear the wisdom of Solomon; and behold, someone greater than Solomon is here.

An unclean spirit returns

"But the unclean spirit, when he is gone out of the man, passes through waterless places, seeking rest, and doesn't find it. Then he says, 'I will return into my house whence I came out,' and when he has come back, he finds it empty, swept, and put in order. Then he goes, and takes with himself seven other spirits more evil than himself, and they enter in and dwell there. The last state of that man becomes worse than the first. Even so will it be also to this evil generation."

Mother and brothers

Source: Mt. 12:46-50

While he was yet speaking to the multitudes, behold, his mother and his brothers stood outside, seeking to speak to him. One said to him, "Behold, your mother and your brothers stand outside, seeking to speak to you."

But he answered him who told him, **"Who is my mother? Who are my brothers?"** He stretched forth his hand towards his disciples, and said, **"Behold, my mother and my brothers! For whoever will do the will of my Father who is in heaven, he is my brother, and sister, and mother."**

— 6 —

A Series of Parables

Jesus is well known for using parables to teach Godly truths. In this chapter He tells a number of them, explicitly explains some, and tells why He uses parables.

The parable of the sower

Location: By Sea of Galilee				Source: Mt. 13:1-17

On that day Jesus went out of the house, and sat by the seaside. Great multitudes gathered to him, so that he entered into a boat, and sat, and all the multitude stood on the beach.

He spoke to them many things in parables, saying, **"Behold, the farmer went forth to sow. As he sowed, some seeds fell by the roadside, and the birds came and devoured them. Others fell on rocky ground, where they didn't have much soil, and immediately they sprang up, because they had no deepness of earth. When the sun had risen, they were scorched. Because they had no root, they withered away. Others fell on thorns. The thorns grew up and choked them: and others fell on good soil, and yielded fruit: some one hundred times, some sixty, and some thirty. He who has ears to hear, let him hear."**

The purpose of parables

The disciples came, and said to him, "Why do you speak to them in parables?"

He answered them, "To you it is given to know the mysteries of the Kingdom of Heaven, but it is not given to them. For whoever has, to him will be given, and he will have abundance, but whoever doesn't have, from him will be taken away even that which he has.

"Therefore I speak to them in parables, because seeing they don't see, and hearing, they don't hear, neither do they understand. In them the prophecy of Isaiah is fulfilled, which says,

'By hearing you will hear, and will in no way understand;
Seeing you will see, and will in no way perceive:
For this people's heart has grown callous,
Their ears are dull of hearing,
Their eyes they have closed;
Or else perhaps they might perceive with their eyes, Hear with their ears,
Understand with their heart, And should turn again;
And I would heal them.'

"But blessed are your eyes, for they see; and your ears, for they hear. For most assuredly I tell you that many prophets and righteous men desired to see the things which you see, and didn't see them; and to hear the things which you hear, and didn't hear them."

Parable of the sower explained
Source: Lk. 8:9; Mk. 4:13; Lk. 8:11; Mt. 13:18-30

Then his disciples asked him, "What does this parable mean?"

He said to them, "Don't you understand this parable? How will you understand all of the parables? Now the parable is this: The seed is the word of God.

"Hear, then, the parable of the farmer. When anyone hears the word of the kingdom, and doesn't understand it, the evil one comes, and snatches away that which has been sown in his heart. This is what was sown by the roadside. What was sown on the rocky places, this is he who hears the word, and immediately with joy receives it; yet he has no root in himself, but endures for a while. When oppression or persecution arises because of the word, immediately he stumbles.

"What was sown among the thorns, this is he who hears the word, but the cares of this world and the deceitfulness of riches choke the word, and he becomes unfruitful. What was sown on the good ground, this is he who hears the word, and understands it, who most assuredly bears fruit, and brings forth, some one hundred times, some sixty, some thirty."

Parable of the wheat and the darnel [or tares]

He set another parable before them, saying, "The Kingdom of Heaven is like a man who sowed good seed in his field, but while people slept, his enemy came and sowed darnel also among the wheat, and went away. But when the blade sprang up and brought forth fruit, then the darnel appeared also.

"The servants of the householder came and said to him, 'Sir, didn't you sow good seed in your field? Where did this darnel come from?' He said to them, 'An enemy has done this.' The servants asked him, 'Do you want us to go and gather them up?' But he said, 'No, lest perhaps while you gather up the darnel, you root up the wheat with them. Let both grow together until the harvest, and in the harvest time I will tell the reapers, "First, gather up the darnel, and bind them in bundles to burn them; but gather the wheat into my barn."'"

Lamp under a basket

Source: Lk. 8:16; Mk. 4:22-32

"No one, when he has lit a lamp, covers it with a container, or puts it under a bed; but puts it on a stand, that those who enter in may see the light. For there is nothing hidden, except that it should be made known; neither was anything made secret, but that it should come to light. If any man has ears to hear, let him hear."

He said to them, "Take heed what you hear. With whatever measure you measure, it will be measured to you, and more will be given to you who hear. For whoever has, to him will more be given, and he who has not, from him will be taken away even that which he has."

The parable of the growing seed

He said, "So is the kingdom of God, as if a man should cast seed on the earth, and should sleep and rise night and day, and the seed should spring up and grow, he doesn't know how. For the earth bears fruit: first the blade, then the ear, then the full grain in the ear. But when the fruit is ripe, immediately he puts forth the sickle, because the harvest has come."

The parable of the mustard seed

He said, "How will we liken the kingdom of God? Or by what parable will we compare it? It is like a grain of mustard seed, which, when it is sown in the earth, though it is less than all the seeds that are on the earth, yet when it is sown, grows up, and becomes greater than all the herbs, and puts out great branches, so that the birds of the sky can lodge under its shadow."

The parable of the Leaven

Source: Mt. 13:33-52

He spoke another parable to them. "The Kingdom of Heaven is like yeast, which a woman took, and hid in three measures of meal, until it was all leavened."

Prophecy and the parables

Jesus spoke all these things in parables to the multitudes; and without a parable, he didn't speak to them, that it might be fulfilled which was spoken through the prophet, saying,

> "I will open my mouth in parables;
> I will utter things hidden from the foundation of the world."[3]

The parable of the darnel explained

Then Jesus sent the multitudes away, and went into the house. His disciples came to him, saying, "Explain to us the parable of the darnel of the field."

He answered them, **"He who sows the good seed is the Son of Man, the field is the world; and the good seed, these are the sons of the kingdom; and the darnel are the sons of the evil one. The enemy who sowed them is the devil. The harvest is the end of the age, and the reapers are angels. As therefore the darnel is gathered up and burned with fire; so will it be in the end of this age.**

"The Son of Man will send forth his angels, and they will gather out of his kingdom all things that cause stumbling, and those who do iniquity, and will cast them into the furnace of fire. There will be weeping and the gnashing of teeth. Then the righteous will shine forth as the sun in the kingdom of their Father. He who has ears to hear, let him hear.

---

[3] Psalm 78:2

The parable of the hidden treasure

"The Kingdom of Heaven is like a treasure hidden in the field, which a man found, and hid. In his joy, he goes and sells all that he has, and buys that field.

The parable of the pearl of great price

"Again, the Kingdom of Heaven is like a man who is a merchant seeking fine pearls, who having found one pearl of great price, he went and sold all that he had, and bought it.

The parable of the dragnet

"Again, the Kingdom of Heaven is like a dragnet, that was cast into the sea, and gathered some fish of every kind, which, when it was filled, they drew up on the beach. They sat down, and gathered the good into containers, but the bad they threw away. So will it be in the end of the world. The angels will come forth, and separate the wicked from among the righteous, and will cast them into the furnace of fire. There will be the weeping and the gnashing of teeth."

Jesus said to them, "Have you understood all these things?"

They answered him, "Yes, Lord."

He said to them, "Therefore, every scribe who has been made a disciple to the Kingdom of Heaven is like a man who is a householder, who brings forth out of his treasure new and old things."

— 7 —

Power over Nature and Death

In this chapter Jesus controls nature and death. He sends out His twelve disciples to heal and teach and warns of persecutions and how to respond to them.

Sea made serene

Location: Sea of Galilee   *Source: Mk. 4:35-5:20*

On that day, when evening had come, he said to them, **"Let's go over to the other side."**

Leaving the multitude, they took him with them, even as he was, in the boat. Other small boats were also with him. There arose a great wind storm, and the waves beat into the boat, so much that the boat was already filled. He himself was in the stern, asleep on the cushion, and they woke him up, and told him, "Teacher, don't you care that we are dying?"

He awoke, and rebuked the wind, and said to the sea, **"Peace! Be still!"** The wind ceased, and there was a great calm.

He said to them, **"Why are you so afraid? How is it that you have no faith?"**

They were greatly afraid, and said to one another, "Who then is this, that even the wind and the sea obey him?"

A demon-possessed man healed

They came to the other side of the sea, into the country of the Gadarenes. When he had come out of the boat, immediately there met him out of the tombs a man with an unclean spirit, who had his dwelling in the tombs. Nobody could bind him any more, not even with chains, because he had been often bound with fetters and chains, and the chains had been torn apart by him, and the fetters broken in pieces. Nobody had the strength to tame him.

Always, night and day, in the tombs and in the mountains, he was crying out, and cutting himself with stones. When he saw Jesus from afar, he ran and bowed down to him, and crying out with a loud voice, he said, "What have I to do with you, Jesus, you Son of the Most High God? I adjure you by God, don't torment me."

For he said to him, **"Come out of the man, you unclean spirit!"** He asked him, **"What is your name?"**

He said to him, "My name is Legion, for we are many." He begged him much that he would not send them away out of the country. Now there was on the mountainside a great herd of pigs feeding. All the demons begged him, saying, "Send us into the pigs, that we may enter into them."

At once Jesus gave them permission. The unclean spirits came out and entered into the pigs. The herd of about two thousand rushed down the steep bank into the sea, and they were drowned in the sea. Those who fed them fled, and told it in the city and in the country. The people came to see what it was that had happened.

They came to Jesus, and saw him who was possessed by demons sitting, clothed, and in his right mind, even him who had the legion; and they were afraid. Those who saw it declared to them how it happened to him who was possessed by demons, and about the pigs. They began to beg him to depart from their borders.

As he was entering into the boat, he who had been possessed by demons begged him that he might be with him. He didn't allow him, but said to him, **"Go to your house, to your friends, and tell them how the Lord has done great things for you, and how he had mercy on you."**

He went his way, and began to proclaim in Decapolis how Jesus had done great things for him, and everyone marveled.

Woman healed and girl restored to life
Source: Mk. 5:21-31; Lk. 8:46; Mk. 5:32;
Lk. 8:47-48; Mk. 5:35-43

When Jesus had crossed back over in the boat to the other side, a great multitude was gathered to him; and he was by the sea. Behold, one of the rulers of the synagogue, Jairus by name, came; and seeing him, he fell at his feet, and begged him much, saying, "My little daughter is at the point of death. Please come and lay your hands on her, that she may be made healthy, and live."

He went with him, and a great multitude followed him, and they pressed upon him on all sides. A certain woman, who had an issue of blood for twelve years, and had suffered many things by many physicians, and had spent all that she had, and was no better, but rather grew worse, having heard the things concerning Jesus, came up behind him in the crowd, and touched his clothes. For she said, "If I just touch his clothes, I will be made well." Immediately the fountain of her blood was dried up, and she felt in her body that she was healed of her plague.

Immediately Jesus, perceiving in himself that the power had gone forth from him, turned around in the crowd, and asked, **"Who touched my clothes?"**

His disciples said to him, "You see the multitude pressing against you, and you say, 'Who touched me?'"

But Jesus said, **"Someone did touch me, for I perceived that power has gone out of me."** He looked around to see her who had done this thing.

When the woman saw that she was not hidden, she came trembling, and falling down before him declared to him in the presence of all the people the reason why she had touched him, and how she was healed immediately.

He said to her, **"Daughter, cheer up. Your faith has made you well. Go in peace."**

While he was still speaking, they came from the synagogue ruler's house saying, "Your daughter is dead. Why bother the Teacher any more?"

But Jesus, not heeding the word spoken, immediately said to the ruler of the synagogue, **"Don't be afraid, only believe."**

He allowed no one to follow him, except Peter, James, and John the brother of James. He came to the synagogue ruler's house, and he saw an uproar, weeping, and great wailing.

When he had entered in, he said to them, **"Why do you make an uproar and weep? The child is not dead, but is asleep."**

They laughed him to scorn. But he, having put them all out, took the father of the child and her mother and those who were with him, and went in where the child was lying. Taking the child by the hand, he said to her, **"Talitha cumi;"** which means, being interpreted, **"Young lady, I tell you, get up."**

Immediately the young lady rose up, and walked, for she was twelve years old. They were amazed with great amazement. He charged them much that no one should know this, and commanded that something should be given to her to eat.

Two blind men healed

Source: Mt. 9:27-34

As Jesus passed by from there, two blind men followed him, calling out and saying, "Have mercy on us, son of David!" When he had come into the house, the blind men came to him.

Jesus said to them, **"Do you believe that I am able to do this?"**

They told him, "Yes, Lord."

Then he touched their eyes, saying, **"According to your faith be it done to you."** Their eyes were opened.

Jesus strictly charged them, saying, **"See that no one knows about this."** But they went out and spread abroad his fame in all that land.

As they went forth, behold, there was brought to him a mute man who was demon possessed. When the demon was cast out, the mute man spoke. The multitudes marveled, saying, "Nothing like this has ever been seen in Israel!" But the Pharisees said, "By the prince of the demons, he casts out demons."[4]

---

[4] Confronted with the reality of such miracles, the Pharisees attributed them to "the ruler of the demons." They would use this accusation repeatedly—that Jesus' powers came not from God, but from the devil.

Jesus rejected for second time at Nazareth

Location: Nazareth   Source: Mk. 6:1-6

He went out from there. He came into his own country, and his disciples followed him. When the Sabbath had come, he began to teach in the synagogue, and many hearing him were astonished, saying, "Where did this man get these things?" and, "What is the wisdom that is given to this man, that such mighty works come about by his hands? Isn't this the carpenter, the son of Mary, and brother of James, Joses, Judas, and Simon? Aren't his sisters here with us?" They were offended by him.

Jesus said to them, **"A prophet is not without honor, except in his own country, and among his own relatives, and in his own house."**

He could do no mighty work there, except that he laid his hands on a few sick folk, and healed them. He marveled because of their unbelief. He went around the villages teaching.

Compassion of Jesus

Source: Mt. 9:35-38; Mt. 10:1-42

Jesus went about all the cities and the villages, teaching in their synagogues, and preaching the gospel of the kingdom, and healing every disease and every sickness among the people. But when he saw the multitudes, he was moved with compassion for them, because they were weary and scattered, as sheep without a shepherd.

Then he said to his disciples, **"The harvest indeed is plentiful, but the laborers are few. Pray therefore that the Lord of the harvest will send forth laborers into his harvest."**

Sending out the twelve disciples

He called to himself his twelve disciples, and gave them authority over unclean spirits, to cast them out, and to heal every disease and every sickness.

Now the names of the twelve apostles are these. The first, Simon, who is called Peter; Andrew, his brother; James the son of Zebedee; John, his brother; Philip; Bartholomew; Thomas; Matthew, the tax collector; James the son of Alphaeus; and Lebbaeus, whose surname was Thaddaeus; Simon the Canaanite; and Judas Iscariot, who also betrayed him.

Jesus sent these twelve forth, and charged them, saying, **"Don't go among the Gentiles, and don't enter into any city of the Samaritans. Rather, go to the lost sheep of the house of Israel.**[5] **As you go, preach, saying, 'The Kingdom of Heaven is at hand.' Heal the sick, cleanse the lepers, and cast out demons. Freely you received, so freely give. Don't take any gold, nor silver, nor brass in your money belts. Take no bag for your journey, neither two coats, nor shoes, nor staff: for the laborer is worthy of his food.**

"Into whatever city or village you enter, find out who in it is worthy; and stay there until you go on. As you enter into the household, greet it. If the household is worthy, let your peace come on it, but if it isn't worthy, let your peace return to you. Whoever doesn't receive you, nor hear your words, as you go forth out of that house or that city, shake off the dust from your feet. Most assuredly I tell you, it will be more tolerable for the land of Sodom and Gomorrah in the day of judgment, than for that city.

---

[5] While on earth, Jesus focused His ministry on the Jews. After His death and resurrection, He gave "the great commission," commanding His disciples to spread the Good News to all the world.

Persecutions are coming

"Behold, I send you forth as sheep in the midst of wolves. Therefore be wise as serpents, and harmless as doves. But beware of men: for they will deliver you up to councils, and in their synagogues they will scourge you. Yes, and you will be brought before governors and kings for my sake, for a testimony to them and to the Gentiles.

"But when they deliver you up, don't be anxious how or what you will say, for it will be given you in that hour what you will say. For it is not you who speak, but the Spirit of your Father who speaks in you. Brother will deliver up brother to death, and the father his child. Children will rise up against parents, and cause them to be put to death. You will be hated by all men for my name's sake, but he who endures to the end, the same will be saved.

"But when they persecute you in this city, flee into the next, for most assuredly I tell you, you will not have gone through the cities of Israel, until the Son of Man has come. A disciple is not above his teacher, nor a servant above his lord. It is enough for the disciple that he be like his teacher, and the servant like his lord.

"If they have called the master of the house Beelzebul, how much more them of his household! Therefore don't be afraid of them, for there is nothing covered, that will not be revealed; and hidden, that will not be known.

Don't be afraid

"What I tell you in the darkness, speak in the light; and what you hear whispered in the ear, proclaim on the housetops. Don't be afraid of those who kill the body, but are not able to kill the soul. Rather, fear him who is able to destroy both soul and body in Gehenna *[Hell]*. Aren't two sparrows sold for an assarion *[a copper coin of low value]*? Not one of them falls on the ground apart from your Father's will, but the very hairs of your head are all numbered. Therefore don't be afraid, you are of more value than many sparrows.

Confess Christ before men

"Everyone therefore who confesses me before men, him will I also confess before my Father who is in heaven. But whoever denies me before men, him will I also deny before my Father who is in heaven.

Christ brings division

"Don't think that I came to send peace on the earth. I didn't come to send peace, but a sword. For I came to set a man at odds against his father, and the daughter against her mother, and the daughter-in-law against her mother-in-law. A man's foes will be those of his own household.

"He who loves father or mother more than me is not worthy of me; and he who loves son or daughter more than me isn't worthy of me. He who doesn't take his cross and follow after me, isn't worthy of me. He who finds his life will lose it; and he who loses his life for my sake will find it.

He who receives you receives me

"He who receives you receives me, and he who receives me receives him who sent me. He who receives a prophet in the name of a prophet will receive a prophet's reward: and he who receives a righteous man in the name of a righteous man will receive a righteous man's reward. Whoever gives one of these little ones just a cup of cold water to drink, in the name of a disciple, most assuredly I tell you he will in no way lose his reward."

— 8 —

Feeding Multitudes

This chapter includes two cases in which Jesus miraculously creates food for large crowds. It also reports His rejection by many. Shortly before the first event in this chapter, Jesus is informed that John the Baptist was beheaded by Herod.

Feeding of the five thousand

Location: Near Bethsaida Source: Mt. 14:13-14 (+Mk. 6:31); Jn. 6:5-7; Mt. 14:15-16; Jn. 6:8-9; Mt. 14:18; Lk. 9:14-16; Jn. 6:12-13; Mt. 14:21; Jn. 6:14

Now when Jesus heard this, he said to them, **"You come apart into a desert place, and rest awhile."**

He withdrew from there in a boat, to a desert place apart. When the multitudes heard it, they followed him on foot from the cities. Jesus went out, and he saw a great multitude. He had compassion on them, and healed their sick.

Jesus therefore lifting up his eyes, and seeing that a great multitude was coming to him, said to Philip, **"Where are we to buy bread, that these may eat?"**

This he said to test him, for he himself knew what he would do. Philip answered him, "Two hundred denarii worth of bread is not sufficient for them, that everyone of them may receive a little."

Feeding Multitudes

When evening had come, his disciples came to him, saying, "The place is a desert, and the time is already past. Send the multitudes away, that they may go into the villages, and buy themselves food."

But Jesus said to them, **"They don't need to go away. You give them something to eat."**

One of his disciples, Andrew, Simon Peter's brother, said to him, "There is a boy here who has five barley loaves and two fish, but what are these among so many?"

He said, **"Bring them here to me."**

They were about five thousand men. He said to his disciples, **"Make them sit down in groups of about fifty each."** They did so, and made them all sit down.

He took the five loaves and the two fish, and looking up to the sky, he blessed them, and broke them, and gave them to the disciples to set before the multitude.

When they *[the multitude]* were filled, he said to his disciples, **"Gather up the broken pieces which are left over, that nothing be lost."**

So they gathered them up, and filled twelve baskets with broken pieces from the five barley loaves, which were left over by those who had eaten. Those who ate were about five thousand men, besides women and children. When therefore the people saw the sign which Jesus did, they said, "This is truly the prophet who comes into the world."

Jesus walks on water

Location: Sea of Galilee   *Source: Mt. 14:22-36*

Immediately Jesus made the disciples get into the boat, and to go ahead of him to the other side, while he sent the multitudes away. After he had sent the multitudes away, he went up into the mountain apart to pray.

When evening had come, he was there alone. But the boat was now in the midst of the sea, distressed by the waves, for the wind was contrary. In the fourth watch of the night Jesus came to them, walking on the sea. When the disciples saw him walking on the sea, they were troubled, saying, "It is a ghost!" and they cried out for fear.

But immediately Jesus spoke to them, saying **"Cheer up! I AM! Don't be afraid."**

Peter answered him and said, "Lord, if it is you, command me to come to you on the waters."

He said, **"Come!"**

Peter went down from the boat, and walked on the waters to come to Jesus. But when he saw that the wind was strong, he was afraid, and beginning to sink, he cried out, saying, "Lord, save me!"

Immediately Jesus stretched forth his hand, and took hold of him, and said to him, **"You of little faith, why did you doubt?"**

When they got up into the boat, the wind ceased. Those who were in the boat came and worshiped him, saying, "You are truly the Son of God!"

Feeding Multitudes

Made well by His touch
Location: Gennesaret

When they had crossed over, they came to the land of Gennesaret. When the men of that place recognized him, they sent into all that region round about, and brought to him all who were sick, and they begged him that they might only touch the fringe of his garment. As many as touched it were made whole.

The bread from heaven
Location: Capernaum   *Source: Jn. 6:22-71,7:1*

On the next day, the multitude that stood on the other side of the sea saw that there was no other boat there, except the one which his disciples had entered, and that Jesus hadn't entered with his disciples into the boat, but his disciples went away alone. However boats from Tiberias came near to the place where they ate the bread after the Lord had given thanks. When the multitude therefore saw that Jesus wasn't there, neither his disciples, they themselves got into the boats, and came to Capernaum, seeking Jesus. When they found him on the other side of the sea, they asked him, "Rabbi, when did you come here?"

Jesus answered them, **"Most assuredly I tell you, you seek me, not because you saw signs, but because you ate of the loaves, and were filled. Don't work for the food which perishes, but for the food which remains to eternal life, which the Son of Man will give to you. For the Father, even God, has sealed him."**

They said therefore to him, "What must we do, that we may work the works of God?"

Jesus answered them, **"This is the work of God, that you believe in him whom he has sent."**

They said therefore to him, "What then do you do for a sign, that we may see, and believe you? What work do you do? Our fathers ate the manna in the wilderness. As it is written, 'He gave them bread out of heaven to eat.'"

Jesus therefore said to them, **"Most assuredly, I tell you, it wasn't Moses who gave you the bread out of heaven, but my Father gives you the true bread out of heaven. For the bread of God is that which comes down out of heaven, and gives life to the world."**

They said therefore to him, "Lord, always give us this bread."

Jesus said to them. **"I am the bread of life. He who comes to me will not be hungry, and he who believes in me will never be thirsty. But I told you that you have seen me, and yet don't believe. All those who the Father gives me will come to me. Him who comes to me I will in no way throw out. For I have come down from heaven, not to do my own will, but the will of him who sent me. This is the will of my Father who sent me, that of all he has given to me I should lose nothing, but should raise them up at the last day. This is the will of the one who sent me, that everyone who sees the Son, and believes in him, should have eternal life; and I will raise him up at the last day."**

Rejected by his own

The Jews therefore murmured concerning him, because he said, "I am the bread which came down out of heaven." They said, "Isn't this Jesus, the son of Joseph, whose father and mother we know? How then does he say, 'I have come down out of heaven?'"

Therefore Jesus answered them, **"Don't murmur among yourselves. No one can come to me unless the Father who sent me draws him, and I will raise him up in the last day. It is written in** the prophets, 'They will all be taught by God.' Therefore everyone who hears from the Father, and has learned, comes to me. Not that any man has seen the Father, except he who is from God. He has seen the Father.

"Most assuredly, I tell you, he who believes in me has eternal life. I am the bread of life. Your fathers ate the manna in the wilderness, and they died. This is the bread which comes down out of heaven, that a man may eat of it, and not die. I am the living bread which came down out of heaven. If anyone eats of this bread, he will live forever. Yes, the bread which I will give is my flesh, for the life of the world."

The Jews therefore contended with one another, saying, "How can this man give us his flesh to eat?"

Jesus therefore said to them, "**Most assuredly I tell you, unless you eat the flesh of the Son of Man and drink his blood, you don't have life in yourselves.** He who eats my flesh and drinks my blood has eternal life, and I will raise him up at the last day. For my flesh is food indeed, and my blood is drink indeed. He who eats my flesh and drinks my blood lives in me, and I in him. As the living Father sent me, and I live because of the Father; so he who feeds on me, he will also live because of me. This is the bread which came down out of heaven — not as our fathers ate the manna, and died. He who eats this bread will live forever."

These things he said in the synagogue, as he taught in Capernaum.

Many disciples turn away
Therefore many of his disciples, when they heard this, said, "This is a hard saying! Who can hear it?"

But Jesus knowing in himself that his disciples murmured at this, said to them, **"Does this cause you to stumble? What if you would see the Son of Man ascending to where he was before? It is the spirit who gives life. The flesh profits nothing. The words that I speak to you are spirit, and are life. But there are some of you who don't believe."**

For Jesus knew from the beginning who they were who didn't believe, and who it was who would betray him.

He said, **"For this cause have I said to you that no one can come to me, unless it is given to him by my Father."**

At this, many of his disciples went back, and walked no more with him.

Jesus said therefore to the twelve, **"You don't also want to go away, do you?"**

Simon Peter answered him, "Lord, to whom would we go? You have the words of eternal life. We have come to believe and know that you are the Christ, the Son of the living God."

Jesus answered them, **"Didn't I choose you, the twelve, and one of you is a devil?"**

Now he spoke of Judas, the son of Simon Iscariot, for it was he who would betray him, being one of the twelve. After these things, Jesus walked in Galilee, for he would not walk in Judea, because the Jews sought to kill him.

Defilement comes from within
Source: Mk. 7:1-16; Mt. 15:12-19; Mk. 7:22; Mt. 15:20

Then the Pharisees, and some of the scribes gathered together to him, having come from Jerusalem. Now when they saw some of his disciples eating bread with defiled, that is, unwashed, hands, they found fault. (For the Pharisees, and all the Jews, don't eat unless they wash their hands and forearms, holding to the tradition of the elders. They don't eat when they come from the marketplace, unless they bathe themselves, and there are many other things, which they have received to hold to: washings of cups, pitchers, bronze vessels, and couches.)

The Pharisees and the scribes asked him, "Why don't your disciples walk according to the tradition of the elders, but eat their bread with unwashed hands?"

He answered them, **"Well did Isaiah prophesy of you hypocrites, as it is written,**

> **'This people honors me with their lips,**
> **But their heart is far from me.**
> **But in vain do they worship me,**
> **Teaching as doctrines the commandments of men.'**[6]

"For you set aside the commandment of God, and hold tightly to the tradition of men — the washing of pitchers and cups, and you do many other such things."

He said to them, "Full well do you reject the commandment of God, that you may keep your tradition. For Moses said, 'Honor your father and your mother;' and, 'He who speaks evil of father or mother, let him be put to death.' But you say, 'If a man will tell his father or his mother, "Whatever you might have been profited by me is Corban, that is to say, given to God;"' and you no longer allow him to do anything for his father or his mother, making void

---

[6] Isaiah 29:13

the word of God by your tradition, which you have handed down.[7] You do many things like this."

He called all the multitude to himself, and said to them, "**Hear me, all of you, and understand.** There is nothing from outside of the man, that going into him can defile him; but the things which proceed out of the man are those that defile the man. If anyone has ears to hear, let him hear!"

Then the disciples came, and said to him, "Do you know that the Pharisees were offended, when they heard this saying?"

But he answered, "**Every plant which my heavenly Father didn't plant will be uprooted. Let them alone. They are blind guides of the blind. If the blind guide the blind, both will fall into a pit.**"

Peter answered him, "Explain the parable to us."

So Jesus said, "**Do you also still not understand? Don't you understand that whatever goes into the mouth passes into the belly, and then out of the body? But the things which proceed out of the mouth come forth out of the heart, and they defile the man.**

"**For out of the heart come forth evil thoughts, murders, adulteries, sexual sins, thefts, false testimony, and blasphemies, covetings, wickedness, deceit, lustful desires, an evil eye, blasphemy, pride, and foolishness. These are the things which defile the man; but to eat with unwashed hands doesn't defile the man.**"

---

[7] Jesus is referring to a practice in those times where some people would dedicate their possessions to God, thus formally escaping having to use their possessions to help others, particularly parents.

Feeding Multitudes

A Gentile shows her faith—daughter healed

Location: Phoenicia
(area of Tyre & Sidon)

Source: Mt. 15:21-25; Mk. 7:26-28;
Mt. 15:28 (+Mk. 7:29)

Jesus went out from there, and withdrew into the parts of Tyre and Sidon. Behold, a Canaanite woman came out from those borders, and cried, saying, "Have mercy on me, Lord, you son of David. My daughter is grievously vexed with a demon."

But he answered her not a word. His disciples came and begged him, saying, "Send her away; for she cries after us."

But he answered, **"I wasn't sent to anyone but the lost sheep of the house of Israel."**

But she came and worshiped him, saying, "Lord, help me." Now the woman was a Greek, a Syrophoenician by race. She begged him that he would cast the demon out of her daughter.

But Jesus said to her, **"Let the children be filled first, for it is not appropriate to take the children's bread and throw it to the dogs."**[8]

But she answered him, "Yes, Lord. For even the dogs under the table eat the children's crumbs."

Then Jesus answered her, **"Woman, great is your faith! Be it done to you even as you desire. For this saying, go your way. The demon has gone out of your daughter."**

And her daughter was healed from that hour.

---

[8] The "children" are the people of Israel; "the dogs" refers to the Gentiles.

Jesus heals great multitudes

Location: Decapolis   Source: Mt. 15:29-31

Jesus departed there, and came near to the sea of Galilee; and he went up into the mountain, and sat there. There came to him great multitudes, having with them the lame, blind, mute, maimed, and many others, and they put them down at his feet. He healed them, so that the multitude wondered, when they saw the mute speaking, the injured whole, lame walking, and the blind seeing — and they glorified the God of Israel.

Jesus heals a deaf mute

Source: Mk. 7:32-37

They brought to him one who was deaf and had an impediment in his speech. They begged him to lay his hand on him. He took him aside from the multitude, privately, and put his fingers into his ears, and he spat, and touched his tongue.

Looking up to heaven, he sighed, and said to him, **"Ephphatha!"** that is, **"Be opened!"**

Immediately his ears were opened, and the impediment of his tongue was loosed, and he spoke clearly. He charged them that they should tell no one, but the more he charged them, so much the more widely they proclaimed it. They were astonished beyond measure, saying, "He has done all things well. He makes even the deaf hear, and the mute speak!"

Feeding of the four thousand

Location: Decapolis   Source: Mk. 8:1-3; Mt. 15:33-39

In those days, when there was a very great multitude, and they had nothing to eat, Jesus called his disciples to himself, and said to them,

Feeding Multitudes

"I have compassion on the multitude, because they continue with me now three days, and have nothing to eat. If I send them away fasting to their home, they will faint on the way, for some of them have come a long way."

The disciples said to him, "Where should we get so many loaves in a desert place as to fill so great a multitude?"

Jesus said to them, **"How many loaves do you have?"**

They said, "Seven, and a few small fish."

He commanded the multitude to sit down on the ground; and he took the seven loaves and the fish. He gave thanks and broke them, and gave to the disciples, and the disciples to the multitudes. They all ate, and were filled. They took up seven baskets full of the broken pieces that were left over.

Those who ate were four thousand men, besides women and children. He sent away the multitudes, and entered into the boat, and came into the borders of Magdala.

— 9 —

Death, Resurrection, Transfiguration

In this chapter, Jesus criticizes the Pharisees and Sadducees who test Him, Peter confesses Jesus is the Christ, Jesus predicts His coming death and resurrection, and Jesus undergoes the famous "transfiguration."

The Pharisees and Sadducees seek a sign

Location: Magdala   Source: *Mt. 16:1; Mk. 8:12; Mt. 16:2-4; Mk. 8:13; Mt. 16:5-8 (+Mk. 8:15); Mk. 8:17-21; Mt. 16:11-12*

The Pharisees and Sadducees came, and testing him, asked him to show them a sign from heaven.

He sighed deeply in his spirit, and said, **"Why does this generation seek a sign? Most assuredly I tell you, there will no sign be given to this generation."**

But he answered them, **"When it is evening, you say, 'It will be fair weather, for the sky is red.' In the morning, 'It will be foul weather today, for the sky is red and threatening.' Hypocrites! You know how to discern the appearance of the sky, but you can't discern the signs of the times. An evil and adulterous generation seeks after a sign, and there will be no sign given to it, but the sign of the prophet Jonah."**

He left them, and again entering into the boat, departed to the other side.

Death, Resurrection, Transfiguration

Beware of the leaven of the Pharisees and Sadducees
The disciples came to the other side and forgot to take bread.

Jesus said to them, "**Take heed and beware of the yeast of the Pharisees and Sadducees and the yeast of Herod.**"

They reasoned among themselves, saying, "We took no bread."

Jesus, perceiving it, said, "**Why do you reason among yourselves, you of little faith, 'because you have brought no bread?' Don't you perceive yet, neither understand? Is your heart still hardened? Having eyes, don't you see? Having ears, don't you hear? Don't you remember? When I broke the five loaves among the five thousand, how many baskets full of broken pieces did you take up?**"

They told him, "Twelve."

"**When the seven loaves fed the four thousand, how many baskets full of broken pieces did you take up?**"

They told him, "Seven."

He asked them, "**Don't you understand, yet? How is it that you don't perceive that I didn't speak to you concerning bread? But beware of the yeast of the Pharisees and Sadducees.**"

Then they understood that he didn't tell them to beware of the yeast of bread, but of the teaching of the Pharisees and Sadducees.

Blind man healed

Location: Bethsaida   Source: Mk. 8:22-26

He came to Bethsaida. They brought a blind man to him, and begged him to touch him. He took hold of the blind man by the hand, and brought him out of the village. When he had spit on his eyes, and laid his hands on him, he asked him if he saw anything. He looked up, and said, "I see men; for I see them like trees walking."

Then again he laid his hands on his eyes. He looked intently, and was restored, and saw everyone clearly.

He sent him away to his house, saying, **"Don't enter into the village, nor tell anyone in the village."**

Peter confesses Jesus as the Christ

Location: Near Caesarea Philippi   Source: Mt. 16:13-19

Now when Jesus came into the parts of Caesarea Philippi,[9] he asked his disciples, saying, **"Who do men say that I, the Son of Man, am?"**

They said, "Some say John the Baptizer, some, Elijah, and others, Jeremiah, or one of the prophets."

He said to them, **"But who do you say that I am?"**

Simon Peter answered, "You are the Christ, the Son of the living God."

Jesus answered him, **"Blessed are you, Simon Bar-jonah, for flesh and blood has not revealed this to you, but my Father who is in heaven. I also tell you, that you are Peter, and on this rock I will**

---

[9] Note: Caesarea Philippi is a different town than Caesarea.

build my assembly, and the gates of Hades will not prevail against it. I will give to you the keys of the Kingdom of Heaven, and whatever you will bind on earth will be bound in heaven; and whatever you will loose on earth will be loosed in heaven."

Jesus predicts his death and resurrection
Source: Mt. 16:20; Lk. 9:22; Mt. 16:21-23

Then he charged the disciples that they should tell no man that he is Jesus the Christ, saying, **"The Son of Man must suffer many things, and be rejected by the elders, chief priests, and scribes, and be killed, and the third day be raised up."**

From that time, Jesus began to show to his disciples that he must go to Jerusalem and suffer many things from the elders, chief priests, and scribes, and be killed, and the third day be raised up.

Peter took him aside, and began to rebuke him, saying, "Far be it from you, Lord! This will never be done to you."

But he turned, and said to Peter, **"Get behind me, Satan! You are a stumbling-block to me, for you are not setting your mind on the things of God, but the things of men."**

True discipleship: take up the cross and follow Him
Source: Mk. 8:34-38; Mt. 16:27-28

He called the multitude to himself with his disciples, and said to them, **"Whoever wants to come after me, let him deny himself, and take up his cross, and follow me. For whoever wants to save his life will lose it; and whoever will lose his life for my sake and the gospel's will save it.**

"For what does it profit a man, to gain the whole world, and forfeit

his life? For what should a man give in exchange for his life? For whoever will be ashamed of me and of my words in this adulterous and sinful generation, the Son of Man also will be ashamed of him, when he comes in the glory of his Father with the holy angels.

"For the Son of Man will come in the glory of his Father with his angels, and then will he render to every man according to his deeds. Most assuredly I tell you, there are some standing here, who will in no way taste of death, until they see the Son of Man coming in his kingdom."

Jesus transfigured on the mount
Location: Unnamed mountain   *Source: Mt. 17:1-13*

After six days, Jesus took with him Peter, James, and John, his brother, and brought them up into a high mountain by themselves. He was transfigured before them. His face shone like the sun, and his garments became white as the light. Behold, there appeared to them Moses and Elijah talking with him. Peter answered, and said to Jesus, "Lord, it is good for us to be here. If you want, let's make three tents here: one for you, one for Moses, and one for Elijah."

While he was still speaking, behold, a bright cloud overshadowed them. Behold, a voice out of the cloud, saying, "This is my beloved Son, in whom I am well pleased. Listen to him." When the disciples heard it, they fell on their faces, and were very afraid.

Jesus came and touched them and said, **"Get up, and don't be afraid."**

Lifting up their eyes, they saw no one, except Jesus alone.

As they were coming down from the mountain, Jesus commanded them, saying, **"Don't tell anyone what you saw, until the Son of Man has risen from the dead."**

Death, Resurrection, Transfiguration

His disciples asked him, saying, "Then why do the scribes say that Elijah must come first?"

Jesus answered them, **"Elijah indeed comes first, and will restore all things, but I tell you that Elijah has come already, and they didn't recognize him, but did to him whatever they wanted to. Even so will the Son of Man also suffer by them."**

Then the disciples understood that he spoke to them of John the Baptizer.

~ 10 ~

Greatness, Offenses, and Forgiveness

Jesus teaches perspective on several topics, including who would be the greatest, the danger of offenses, forgiveness, and the cost of discipleship.

Epileptic healed

Location: near the mountain of transfiguration   *Source: Mk. 9:14-18; Mt. 17:17; Mk. 9:20-27; Mt. 17:19-21*

Coming to the disciples, he saw a great multitude around them, and scribes questioning them. Immediately all the multitude, when they saw him, were greatly amazed, and running to him greeted him.

He asked the scribes, **"What are you asking them?"**

One of the multitude answered, "Teacher, I brought to you my son, who has a mute spirit; and wherever it seizes him, it dashes him down, and he foams at the mouth, and grinds his teeth, and wastes away. I asked your disciples to cast it out, and they weren't able."

Jesus answered, **"Faithless and perverse generation! How long will I be with you? How long will I bear with you? Bring him here to me."**

They brought him to him *[Jesus]*, and when he saw him, immediately the spirit convulsed him, and he fell on the ground, wallowing and foaming at the mouth.

He asked his father, **"How long has it been since this has come to him?"**

He said, "From childhood. Often it has cast him both into the fire and into the water, to destroy him. But if you can do anything, have compassion on us, and help us."

Jesus said to him, **"If you can believe? All things are possible to him who believes."**

Immediately the father of the child cried out with tears, "I believe. Help my unbelief!"

When Jesus saw that a multitude came running together, he rebuked the unclean spirit, saying to him, **"You mute and deaf spirit, I command you, come out of him, and enter no more into him!"**

Having cried out, and convulsed greatly, it came out of him. The boy became like one dead; so much that most of them said, "He is dead." But Jesus took him by the hand, and raised him up; and he arose.

Then the disciples came to Jesus privately, and said, "Why were we not able to cast it out?"

He said to them, **"Because of your unbelief. For most assuredly I tell you, if you have faith as a grain of mustard seed, you will tell this mountain, 'Move from here to there,' and it will move; and nothing will be impossible to you. But this kind doesn't go out except by prayer and fasting."**

Jesus again predicts His death and resurrection
Location: Galilee *Source: Mt. 17:22; Lk. 9:43-44; Mt. 17:23; Lk. 9:45*

While they were staying in Galilee, Jesus said to his disciples, **"Let these words sink into your ears, for the Son of Man will be delivered up into the hands of men and they will kill him, and the third day he will be raised up."**

They were exceedingly sorry. But they didn't understand this saying. It was concealed from them, that they should not perceive it, and they were afraid to ask him about this saying.

Temple tax paid
Location: Capernaum *Source: Mt. 17:24-27*

When they were come to Capernaum, those who collected the didrachmas *[the temple tax]* came to Peter, and said, "Doesn't your teacher pay the didrachma?" He said, "Yes."

When he came into the house, Jesus anticipated him, saying, **"What do you think, Simon? From whom do the kings of the earth receive toll or tribute? From their sons, or from strangers?"**

Peter said to him, "From strangers."

Jesus said to him, **"Therefore the sons are exempt. But, lest we cause them to stumble, go to the sea, and cast a hook, and take up the first fish that comes up. When you have opened his mouth, you will find a stater** *[an amount of money].* **Take that, and give it to them for me and you."**

Greatness, Offenses, and Forgiveness

Who is the greatest

Location: Capernaum *Source: Mk. 9:33-37; Lk. 9:48; Mt. 18:3-5*

He came to Capernaum, and when he was in the house he asked them, **"What were you arguing among yourselves on the way?"**

But they were silent, for they had disputed one with another on the way about who was the greatest.

He sat down, and called the twelve; and he said to them, **"If any man wants to be first, he will be last of all, and servant of all."**

He took a little child, and set him in the midst of them. Taking him in his arms, he said to them, **"Whoever receives one such little child in my name, receives me, and whoever receives me, doesn't receive me, but him who sent me. For whoever is least among you all, this one will be great.**

"Most assuredly I tell you, unless you turn, and become as little children, you will in no way enter into the Kingdom of Heaven. Whoever therefore will humble himself as this little child, the same is the greatest in the Kingdom of Heaven. Whoever will receive one such little child in my name receives me.

Jesus warns of offenses

Source: Mt. 18:6-7; Mk. 9:43-50

"But whoever will cause one of these little ones who believe in me to stumble, it would be better for him that a huge millstone should be hung around his neck, and that he should be sunk in the depths of the sea. Woe to the world because of occasions of stumbling! For it must be that the occasions come, but woe to that person through whom the occasion comes!

"If your hand causes you to stumble, cut it off. It is better for you to enter into life maimed, rather than having your two hands to go into Gehenna *[Hell]*, into the unquenchable fire,

> 'where their worm doesn't die,
> and the fire is not quenched.'

"If your foot causes you to stumble, cut it off. It is better for you to enter into life lame, rather than having your two feet to be cast into Gehenna, into the fire that will never be quenched —

> 'where their worm doesn't die,
> and the fire is not quenched.'

"If your eye causes you to stumble, cast it out. It is better for you to enter into the kingdom of God with one eye, rather than having two eyes to be cast into the Gehenna of fire,

> 'where their worm doesn't die,
> and the fire is not quenched.'

"For everyone will be salted with fire, and every sacrifice will be seasoned with salt. Salt is good, but if the salt has lost its saltiness, with what will you season it? Have salt in yourselves, and be at peace with one another.

The parable of the lost sheep

Source: Mt. 18:10-14

"See that you don't despise one of these little ones, for I tell you that in heaven their angels always see the face of my Father who is in heaven. For the Son of Man came to save that which was lost.

"What do you think? If a man has one hundred sheep, and one of them goes astray, doesn't he leave the ninety-nine, go to the mountains, and seek that which has gone astray? If he happens to find it, most assuredly I tell you, he rejoices over it more than over the ninety-nine which have not gone astray. Even so it is not the will of your Father who is in heaven that one of these little ones should perish.

Dealing with a sinning brother
Source: Mt. 18:15-20

"If your brother sins against you, go, show him his fault between you and him alone. If he listens to you, you have gained back your brother. But if he doesn't listen, take one or two more with you, that at the mouth of two or three witnesses every word may be established.

"If he refuses to listen to them, tell it to the assembly *[the church]*. If he refuses to hear the assembly also, let him be to you as a Gentile or a tax collector. Most assuredly I tell you, whatever things you will bind on earth will be bound in heaven, and whatever things you will loose on earth will be loosed in heaven.

"Again, assuredly I tell you, that if two of you will agree on earth concerning anything that they will ask, it will be done for them by my Father who is in heaven. For where two or three are gathered together in my name, there I am in the midst of them."

Jesus forbids sectarianism
Source: Mk. 9:38-41

John said to him, "Teacher, we saw someone who doesn't follow us casting out demons in your name; and we forbade him, because he doesn't follow us."

But Jesus said, "Don't forbid him, for there is no one who will do a mighty work in my name, and be able quickly to speak evil of me. For whoever is not against us is on our side. For whoever will give you a cup of water to drink in my name, because you are Christ's, most assuredly I tell you, he will in no way lose his reward."

Forgiveness and the parable of the unforgiving servant
Source: Mt. 18:21-35

Then Peter came and said to him, "Lord, how often will my brother sin against me, and I forgive him? Until seven times?"

Jesus said to him, "I don't tell you until seven times, but, until seventy times seven. Therefore the Kingdom of Heaven is like a certain king, who wanted to reconcile accounts with his servants. When he had begun to reconcile, one was brought to him who owed him ten thousand talents.

"But because he couldn't pay, his lord commanded him to be sold, with his wife, his children, and all that he had, and payment to be made. The servant therefore fell down and kneeled before him, saying, 'Lord, have patience with me, and I will repay you all.' The lord of that servant, being moved with compassion, released him, and forgave him the debt.

"But that servant went out, and found one of his fellow-servants, who owed him one hundred denarii, and he laid hold on him, and took him by the throat, saying, 'Pay me what you owe!' So his fellow-servant fell down at his feet and begged him, saying, 'Have patience with me, and I will repay you.' He would not, but went and cast him into prison, until he should pay back that which was due.

"So when his fellow-servants saw what was done, they were exceedingly sorry, and came and told to their lord all that was done. Then his lord called him in, and said to him, 'You wicked servant! I forgave you all that debt, because you begged me. Shouldn't you also have had mercy on your fellow-servant, even as I had mercy on you?' His lord was angry, and delivered him to the tormentors, until he should pay all that was due to him.

"So will my heavenly Father also do to you, if you don't each forgive his brother from your hearts for his misdeeds."

Jesus' brothers disbelieve
Location: Galilee   *Source: Jn. 7:2-9*

Now the feast of the Jews, the Feast of Booths, was at hand. His brothers therefore said to him, "Depart from here, and go into Judea, that your disciples also may see your works which you do. For no man does anything in secret, and himself seeks to be known openly. If you do these things, reveal yourself to the world." For even his brothers didn't believe in him.

Jesus therefore said to them, **"My time has not yet come, but your time is always ready. The world can't hate you, but it hates me, because I testify about it, that its works are evil. You go up to the feast. I am not yet going up to this feast, because my time is not yet fulfilled."**

Having said these things to them, he stayed in Galilee.

Jesus leaves Galilee for Jerusalem; is rejected by Samaritan village
Source: Lk. 9:51-62

It came to pass, when the days were near that he should be taken up, he intently set his face to go to Jerusalem, and sent messengers before his face. They went, and entered into a village of the Samaritans, so as to prepare for him.

They didn't receive him, because he was traveling with his face set towards Jerusalem. When his disciples, James and John, saw this, they said, "Lord, do you want us to command fire to come down from the sky, and destroy them, just as Elijah did?"

But he turned and rebuked them, **"You don't know what kind of spirit you are of. For the Son of Man didn't come to destroy men's lives, but to save them."**

They went to another village.

Cost of discipleship

As they went on the way, a certain man said to him, "I want to follow you wherever you go, Lord."

Jesus said to him, **"The foxes have holes, and the birds of the sky have nests, but the Son of Man has no place to lay his head."**

He said to another, **"Follow me."**

But he said, "Lord, allow me first to go and bury my father."

But Jesus said to him, **"Leave the dead to bury their own dead, but you go and announce the kingdom of God."**

Another also said, "I want to follow you, Lord, but first allow me to bid farewell to those who are at my house."

But Jesus said to him, **"No one, having put his hand to the plow, and looking back, is fit for the kingdom of God."**

~ 11 ~

Go and Sin No More

This chapter includes the famous story of Jesus telling the adulteress to go and sin no more, His proclamation that "the truth will make you free," and His parable of the good shepherd.

The Feast of Tabernacles in Jerusalem

Location: Jerusalem *Source: Jn. 7:10-53, 8:1*

But when his brothers had gone up to the feast, then he also went up, not publicly, but as it were in secret. The Jews therefore sought him at the feast, and said, "Where is he?" There was much murmuring among the multitudes concerning him. Some said, "He is a good man." Others said, "Not so, but he leads the multitude astray."

Yet no one spoke openly of him for fear of the Jews. But when it was now the midst of the feast, Jesus went up into the temple and taught. The Jews therefore marveled, saying, "How does this man know letters, having never been educated?"

Jesus therefore answered them, **"My teaching is not mine, but his who sent me. If anyone desires to do his will, he will know of the teaching, whether it is from God, or if I speak from myself. He who speaks from himself seeks his own glory, but he who seeks the glory of him who sent him, the same is true, and no unrighteousness is in him. Didn't Moses give you the law, and yet none of you keeps the law? Why do you seek to kill me?"**

The multitude answered, "You have a demon! Who seeks to kill you?"

Jesus answered them, **"I did one work, and you all marvel because of it. Moses has given you circumcision (not that it is of Moses, but of the fathers), and on the Sabbath you circumcise a boy. If a boy receives circumcision on the Sabbath, that the law of Moses may not be broken, are you angry with me, because I made a man every bit whole on the Sabbath? Don't judge according to appearance, but judge righteous judgment."**

Some therefore of them of Jerusalem said, "Isn't this he whom they seek to kill? Behold, he speaks openly, and they say nothing to him. Can it be that the rulers indeed know that this is truly the Christ? However we know where this man comes from, but when the Christ comes, no one will know where he comes from."

Jesus therefore cried out in the temple, teaching and saying, **"You both know me, and know where I am from. I have not come of myself, but he who sent me is true, whom you don't know. I know him, because I am from him, and he sent me."**

They sought therefore to take him. No one laid a hand on him, because his hour had not yet come. But of the multitude, many believed in him. They said, "When the Christ comes, will he do more signs than those which this man has done?" The Pharisees heard the multitude murmuring these things concerning him, and the chief priests and the Pharisees sent officers to arrest him.

Then Jesus said, **"Yet a little while, am I with you, then I go to him who sent me. You will seek me, and won't find me; and where I am, you can't come."**

The Jews therefore said among themselves, "Where will this man go that we won't find him? Will he go to the Dispersion among the Greeks, and teach the Greeks? What is this word that he said, 'You will seek me, and won't find me; and where I am, you can't come?'"

The promise of the Holy Spirit
Now on the last and greatest day of the feast, Jesus stood and cried out, **"If anyone is thirsty, let him come to me and drink! He who believes in me, as the Scripture has said, from within him will flow rivers of living water."**

But he said this about the Spirit, which those believing in him were to receive. For the Holy Spirit was not yet given, because Jesus wasn't yet glorified.

Many of the multitude therefore, when they heard these words, said, "This is truly the prophet." Others said, "This is the Christ." But some said, "What, does the Christ come out of Galilee? Hasn't the Scripture said that the Christ comes of the seed of David, and from Bethlehem, the village where David was?" So there arose a division in the multitude because of him. Some of them would have arrested him, but no one laid hands on him.

The officers therefore came to the chief priests and Pharisees, and they said to them, "Why didn't you bring him?" The officers answered, "No man ever spoke like this man!" The Pharisees therefore answered them, "Are you also led astray? Have any of the rulers believed in him, or of the Pharisees? But this multitude that doesn't know the law is accursed."

Nicodemus (he who came to him by night, being one of them) said to them, "Does our law judge a man, unless it first hears from him personally and knows what he does?"

They answered him, "Are you also from Galilee? Search, and see that no prophet has arisen out of Galilee."

Everyone went to his own house, but Jesus went to the Mount of Olives.

Forgiveness of Adulteress

Location: Jerusalem *Source: Jn. 8:2-12*

At dawn, he came again into the temple, and all the people came to him. He sat down, and taught them. The scribes and the Pharisees brought a woman taken in adultery. Having set her in the midst, they told him, "Teacher, we found this woman in adultery, in the very act. Now in our law, Moses commanded us to stone such. What then do you say about her?"

They said this testing him, that they might have something to accuse him of. But Jesus stooped down, and wrote on the ground with his finger, as if he didn't hear.

But when they continued asking him, he lifted himself up, and said to them, **"He who is without sin among you, let him throw the first stone at her."**

Again he stooped down, and with his finger wrote on the ground. They, when they heard it, being convicted by their conscience, went out one by one, beginning from the oldest, even to the last. Jesus was left alone with the woman where she was, in the middle.

Jesus lifted himself up, and seeing no one but the woman, said to her, **"Woman, where are they? Did no one condemn you?"**

She said, "No one, Lord."

Go and Sin No More

Jesus said, **"Neither do I condemn you. Go your way. From now on, sin no more."**

Again, therefore, Jesus spoke to them, saying, **"I am the light of the world. He who follows me will not walk in the darkness, but will have the light of life."**

Jesus defends his self-witness
Source: Jn. 8:13-59

The Pharisees therefore said to him, "You testify about yourself. Your testimony is not valid."

Jesus answered them, **"Even if I testify about myself, my testimony is true, for I know where I came from, and where I am going; but you don't know where I came from, or where I am going. You judge according to the flesh. I judge no one. Even if I do judge, my judgment is true, for I am not alone, but I am with the Father who sent me. It's also written in your law that the testimony of two men is valid. I am he who testifies about myself, and the Father who sent me testifies about me."**

They said therefore to him, "Where is your Father?"

Jesus answered, **"You know neither me, nor my Father. If you knew me, you would know my Father also."**

Jesus spoke these words in the treasury, as he taught in the temple. No one arrested him, because his hour had not yet come.

Jesus predicts His departure

Jesus said therefore again to them, **"I am going away, and you will seek me, and will die in your sins. Where I go, you can't come."**

The Jews therefore said, "Will he kill himself, that he says, **'Where I am going, you can't come?'"**

He said to them, **"You are from beneath. I am from above. You are of this world. I am not of this world. I said therefore to you that you will die in your sins; for unless you believe that I am he, you will die in your sins."**

They said therefore to him, "Who are you?"

Jesus said to them, **"Just what I have been saying to you from the beginning. I have many things to speak and to judge concerning you. However he who sent me is true; and the things which I heard from him, these I say to the world."**

They didn't perceive that he spoke to them about the Father.

Jesus therefore said to them, **"When you have lifted up the Son of Man, then you will know that I am he, and that I do nothing of myself, but as my Father taught me, I say these things. He who sent me is with me. The Father hasn't left me alone, for I always do the things that are pleasing to him."**

The truth will make you free

As he spoke these things, many believed in him. Jesus therefore said to those Jews who had believed him, **"If you remain in my word, then you are truly my disciples. You will know the truth, and the truth will make you free."**

They answered him, "We are Abraham's seed, and have never yet been in bondage to anyone. How do you say, 'You will be made free?'"

Jesus answered them, **"Most assuredly I tell you, everyone who com-**

Go and Sin No More

mits sin is the bondservant of sin. A bondservant doesn't live in the house forever. A son remains forever. If therefore the Son makes you free, you will be free indeed.

"I know that you are Abraham's seed, yet you seek to kill me, because my word finds no place in you. I say the things which I have seen with my Father; and you also do the things which you have seen with your father."

They answered him, "Our father is Abraham."

Jesus said to them, "If you were Abraham's children, you would do the works of Abraham. But now you seek to kill me, a man who has told you the truth, which I heard from God. Abraham didn't do this. You do the works of your father."

They said to him, "We were not born of sexual immorality. We have one Father, God."

Therefore Jesus said to them, "If God were your Father, you would love me, for I came forth and have come from God. For neither have I come of myself, but he sent me. Why don't you understand my speech? Because you can't hear my word.

"You are of your father, the devil, and you want to do the desires of your father. He was a murderer from the beginning, and doesn't stand in the truth, because there is no truth in him. When he speaks a lie, he speaks on his own; for he is a liar, and the father of it. But because I tell the truth, you don't believe me. Which of you convicts me of sin? If I tell the truth, why do you not believe me? He who is of God hears the words of God. For this cause you don't hear, because you are not of God."

Then the Jews answered him, "Don't we say well that you are a Samaritan, and have a demon?"

Jesus answered, **"I don't have a demon, but I honor my Father, and you dishonor me. But I don't seek my own glory. There is one who seeks and judges. Most assuredly, I tell you, if a person keeps my word, he will never see death."**

Then the Jews said to him, "Now we know that you have a demon. Abraham died, and the prophets; and you say, 'If a man keeps my word, he will never taste of death.' Are you greater than our father, Abraham, who died? The prophets died. Who do you make yourself out to be?"

Jesus answered, **"If I glorify myself, my glory is nothing. It is my Father who glorifies me, of whom you say that he is our God. You have not known him, but I know him. If I said, 'I don't know him,' I would be like you, a liar. But I know him, and keep his word. Your father Abraham rejoiced to see my day. He saw it, and was glad."**

The Jews therefore said to him, "You are not yet fifty years old, and have you seen Abraham?"

Jesus said to them, **"Most assuredly, I tell you, before Abraham was born, I AM."**[10]

They took up stones therefore to throw at him, but Jesus hid himself, and went out of the temple, going through the midst of them, and so passed by.

---

[10] "I AM" is how God referred to Himself when answering Moses (Exodus 3:14). Hence, Jesus was calling Himself God. To the Jews present, this was blasphemy, and so they attempted to stone Him.

Go and Sin No More

A man born blind is healed

Source: Jn. 9:1-41

As he passed by, he saw a man blind from his birth. His disciples asked him, "Rabbi, who sinned, this man or his parents, that he was born blind?"

Jesus answered, **"Neither did this man sin, nor his parents. But, that the works of God might be revealed in him, I must work the works of him who sent me, while it is day. The night is coming, when no one can work. When I am in the world, I am the light of the world."**

When he had said this, he spat on the ground, made mud with the saliva, anointed the blind man's eyes with the mud, and said to him, **"Go, wash in the pool of Siloam"** (which means "Sent").

So he went away, washed, and came seeing. The neighbors therefore, and those who saw that he was blind before, said, "Isn't this he who sat and begged?" Others said, "It is he." Still others said, "He is like him." He said, "I am he." They said therefore to him, "How were your eyes opened?"

He answered, "A man called Jesus made mud, anointed my eyes, and said to me, "Go to the pool of Siloam, and wash." So I went away and washed, and I received sight." Then they asked him, "Where is he?" He said, "I don't know."

The following text from John 9:13-34 contains no words of Jesus, but is important as transition between the previous passage, and what follows next. It also is another illustration of how the Pharisees were troubled over Jesus and His actions.

They brought him who before was blind to the Pharisees. It was a

Sabbath when Jesus made the mud and opened his eyes. Again therefore the Pharisees also asked him how he received his sight. He said to them, "He put mud on my eyes, I washed, and I see." Some therefore of the Pharisees said, "This man is not from God, because he doesn't keep the Sabbath."[11]

Others said, "How can a man who is a sinner do such signs?" There was division among them. Therefore they asked the blind man again, "What do you say about him, in that he opened your eyes?" He said, "He is a prophet." The Jews therefore did not believe concerning him, that he had been blind, and had received his sight, until they called the parents of him who had received his sight, and asked them, "Is this your son, who you say was born blind? How then does he now see?"

His parents answered them, "We know that this is our son, and that he was born blind; but how he now sees, we don't know; or who opened his eyes, we don't know. He is of age. Ask him. He will speak for himself."

His parents said these things because they feared the Jews; for the Jews had already agreed that if any man would confess him as Christ, he would be put out of the synagogue. Therefore his parents said, "He is of age. Ask him." So they called the man who was blind a second time, and said to him, "Give glory to God. We know that this man is a sinner."

He therefore answered, "I don't know if he is a sinner. One thing I know: that though I was blind, now I see." They said to him again, "What did he do to you? How did he open your eyes?" He answered them, "I told you already, and you didn't listen. Why do you want to

---

[11] The Pharisees again were focused on their many man-made rules that had grown up over time, forbidding almost any kind of "work" on the Sabbath, including healing.

hear it again? Do you also want to become his disciples?"

They became abusive towards him and said, "You are his disciple, but we are disciples of Moses. We know that God has spoken to Moses. But as for this man, we don't know where he comes from."

The man answered them, "How amazing! You don't know where he comes from, yet he opened my eyes. We know that God doesn't listen to sinners, but if anyone is a worshipper of God, and does his will, he listens to him. Since the world began it has never been heard of that anyone opened the eyes of a man born blind. If this man were not from God, he could do nothing."

They answered him, "You were altogether born in sins, and do you teach us?" They threw him out.

True vision and blindness
Jesus heard that they had thrown him out, and finding him, he said, **"Do you believe in the Son of God?"**

He answered, "Who is he, Lord, that I may believe in him?"

Jesus said to him, **"You have both seen him, and it is he who speaks with you."**

He said, "Lord, I believe!" and he worshiped him.

Jesus said, **"I came into this world for judgment, that those who don't see may see; and that those who see may become blind."**

Those of the Pharisees who were with him heard these things, and said to him, "Are we also blind?"

Jesus said to them, "**If you were blind, you would have no sin; but now you say, 'We see.' Therefore your sin remains.**

The parable of the good shepherd
(Jesus the True Shepherd)

Location: Jerusalem   Source: Jn. 10:1-21

"Most assuredly, I tell you, he who doesn't enter by the door into the sheep fold, but climbs up some other way, the same is a thief and a robber. But he who enters in by the door is the shepherd of the sheep. The gatekeeper opens the gate for him, and the sheep listen to his voice. He calls his own sheep by name, and leads them out. Whenever he brings out his own sheep, he goes before them, and the sheep follow him, for they know his voice. They will by no means follow a stranger, but will flee from him; for they don't know the voice of strangers."

Jesus spoke this parable to them, but they didn't understand what he was telling them.

Jesus therefore said to them again, "Most assuredly, I tell you, I am the sheep's door. All who came before me are thieves and robbers, but the sheep didn't listen to them. I am the door. If anyone enters in by me, he will be saved, and will go in and go out, and will find pasture. The thief only comes to steal, kill, and destroy. I came that they may have life, and may have it abundantly.

"I am the good shepherd. The good shepherd lays down his life for the sheep. He who is a hired hand, and not a shepherd, who doesn't own the sheep, sees the wolf coming, leaves the sheep, and flees. The wolf snatches the sheep, and scatters them. The hired hand flees because he is a hired hand, and doesn't care for the sheep.

"I am the good shepherd. I know my own, and I'm known by my own; even as the Father knows me, and I know the Father. I lay down my life for the sheep. I have other sheep, which are not of this fold. I must bring them also, and they will hear my voice. They will become one flock with one shepherd.

"Therefore the Father loves me, because I lay down my life, that I may take it again. No one takes it away from me, but I lay it down by myself. I have power to lay it down, and I have power to take it again. I received this commandment from my Father."

Therefore a division arose again among the Jews because of these words. Many of them said, "He has a demon, and is mad! Why do you listen to him?" Others said, "These are not the sayings of one possessed by a demon. It isn't possible for a demon to open the eyes of the blind, is it?"

The seventy sent out

Location: Probably Judea *Source: Lk. 10:1-24*

Now after these things the Lord also appointed seventy others, and sent them two by two before his face into every city and place, where he himself was about to come.[12]

Then he said to them, "**The harvest is indeed plentiful, but the laborers are few. Pray therefore to the Lord of the harvest, that he may send out laborers into his harvest. Go your ways. Behold, I send you out as lambs in the midst of wolves. Carry no purse, nor wallet, nor sandals. Greet no one on the way. Into whatever house you enter, first say, 'Peace be to this house.'**

---

[12] This is a different event from the "sending out of the twelve," described previously, although the instructions are similar. It's very plausible that similar instructions would be given for a similar mission. (And Luke's Gospel records both events separately.)

"If a son of peace is there, your peace will rest on him; but if not, it will return to you. Remain in that same house, eating and drinking the things they give, for the laborer is worthy of his wages. Don't go from house to house. Into whatever city you enter, and they receive you, eat the things that are set before you. Heal the sick who are therein, and tell them, 'The kingdom of God has come near to you.'

"But into whatever city you enter, and they don't receive you, go out into the streets of it and say, 'Even the dust from your city that clings to us, we wipe off against you. Nevertheless know this, that the kingdom of God has come near to you.' I tell you, it will be more tolerable in that day for Sodom than for that city.

Woe to the impenitent cities[13]

"Woe to you, Chorazin! Woe to you, Bethsaida! For if the mighty works had been done in Tyre and Sidon which were done in you, they would have repented long ago, sitting in sackcloth and ashes. But it will be more tolerable for Tyre and Sidon in the judgment than for you. You, Capernaum, who are exalted to heaven, will be brought down to Hades. Whoever listens to you listens to me, and whoever rejects you rejects me. Whoever rejects me rejects him who sent me."

The seventy return with joy

The seventy returned with joy, saying, "Lord, even the demons are subject to us in your name."

---

[13] These words are almost exactly the same as quoted previously but are repeated on this different occasion. It is not unusual that Jesus (or anyone) might repeat things considered important on more than one occasion, perhaps many times.

He said to them, "I saw Satan having fallen like lightning from heaven. Behold, I give you authority to tread on serpents and scorpions, and over all the power of the enemy. Nothing will in any way hurt you. Nevertheless, don't rejoice in this, that the spirits are subject to you, but rejoice that your names are written in heaven."

Jesus rejoices in the Holy Spirit

In that same hour Jesus rejoiced in the Holy Spirit, and said, "I thank you, O Father, Lord of heaven and earth, that you have hidden these things from the wise and understanding, and revealed them to little children. Yes, Father, for so it was well-pleasing in your sight."

Turning to the disciples, he said, "All things have been delivered to me from my Father. No one knows who the Son is, except the Father, and who the Father is, except the Son, and he to whoever the Son desires to reveal him."

Turning to the disciples, he said privately, "Blessed are the eyes which see the things that you see, for I tell you that many prophets and kings desired to see the things which you see, and didn't see them, and to hear the things which you hear, and didn't hear them."

— 12 —

The Good Samaritan; Persistence in Prayer

This chapter includes the famous parable of the good Samaritan, instruction to be persistence in prayer, and not to worry.

The parable of the good Samaritan

Location: Possibly Judea　　　　　　　　　Source: Lk. 10:25-42

Behold, a certain lawyer stood up and tested him, saying, "Teacher, what will I do to inherit eternal life?"

He said to him, **"What is written in the law? How do you read it?"**

He answered, "You shall love the Lord your God with all your heart, with all your soul, with all your strength, and with all your mind; and your neighbor as yourself."

He said to him, **"You have answered correctly. Do this, and you will live."**

But he, desiring to justify himself, asked Jesus, "Who is my neighbor?"

Jesus answered, **"A certain man was going down from Jerusalem to Jericho, and he fell among robbers, who both stripped him and beat him, and departed, leaving him half dead. By chance a certain** priest was going down that way. When he saw him, he passed by on the other side. In the same way a Levite also, when he came to the place, and saw him, passed by on the other side.

"But a certain Samaritan, as he journeyed, came where he was. When he saw him, he was moved with compassion, came to him, and bound up his wounds, pouring on oil and wine. He set him on his own animal, and brought him to an inn, and took care of him. On the next day, when he departed, he took out two denarii, and gave them to the host, and said to him, 'Take care of him. Whatever you spend beyond that, I will repay you when I return.' Now which of these three do you think seemed to be a neighbor to him who fell among the robbers?"

He said, "He who shown mercy on him."

Then Jesus said to him, **"Go and do likewise."**

Martha and Mary worship and serve Jesus

Location: Bethany

It happened as they went on their way, he entered into a certain village, and a certain woman named Martha received him into her house. She had a sister called Mary, who also sat at Jesus' feet, and heard his word. But Martha was distracted with much serving, and she came up to him, and said, "Lord, don't you care that my sister left me to serve alone? Ask her therefore to help me."

Jesus answered her, **"Martha, Martha, you are anxious and troubled about many things, but one thing is needed. Mary has chosen the good part, which will not be taken away from her."**

Lessons on prayer: "The Lord's Prayer"

Location: Judea possibly Source: Lk. 11:1-13

It happened, that when he finished praying in a certain place, one of his disciples said to him, "Lord, teach us to pray, just as John also taught his disciples."

He said to them, **"When you pray, say,**[14]**"**

> **'Our Father in heaven,**
> **May your name be kept holy.**
> **May your kingdom come.**
> **May your desire be done on Earth, as it is in heaven.**
> **Give us day by day our daily bread.**
> **Forgive us our sins,**
> **For we ourselves also forgive everyone who is indebted to us.**
> **Bring us not into temptation,**
> **But deliver us from the evil one.'"**

Lessons on prayer: be persistent

He said to them, **"Which of you, if you go to a friend at midnight, and tell him, 'Friend, lend me three loaves of bread, for a friend of mine has come to me from a journey, and I have nothing to set before him,' and he from within will answer and say, 'Don't bother me. The door is now shut, and my children are with me in bed. I can't get up and give it to you'? I tell you, although he will not rise and give it to him because he is his friend, yet because of his persistence, he will get up and give him as many as he needs.**

---

[14] This wording of the Lord's Prayer is slightly different than the one Jesus gave during the Sermon on the Mount. In both cases He is giving a model outline for prayer.

"I tell you, keep asking, and it will be given you. Keep seeking, and you will find. Keep knocking, and it will be opened to you. For everyone who asks receives. He who seeks finds. To him who knocks it will be opened. Which of you fathers, if your son asks for bread, will give him a stone? Or if he asks for a fish, he won't give him a snake instead of a fish, will he? Or if he asks for an egg, he won't give him a scorpion, will he? If you then, being evil, know how to give good gifts to your children, how much more will your heavenly Father give the Holy Spirit to those who ask him?"[15]

Accused of casting out Demons by Beelzebul
Source: Lk. 11:14-32

[Note: These verses Lk. 11:14-32 are highly similar to those in Mt. 12:22-45 (as found in chapter 5 of this book), but likely represent a different but similar situation. See Appendix for discussion.]

He was casting out a demon, and it was mute. It happened, when the demon had gone out, the mute man spoke; and the multitudes marveled. But some of them said, "He casts out demons by Beelzebul, the prince of the demons." Others, testing him, sought from him a sign from heaven.

But he, knowing their thoughts, said to them, **"Every kingdom divided against itself is brought to desolation. A house divided against itself falls. If Satan also is divided against himself, how will his kingdom stand? Because you say that I cast out demons by Beelzebul. But if I cast out demons by Beelzebul, by whom do your sons cast them out? Therefore will they be your judges. But if I by the finger of God cast out demons, then the kingdom of God has come to you.**

---

[15] This paragraph is very close to what Jesus said before in the Sermon on the Mount. He gave many of His teachings more than once.

"When the strong man, fully armed, guards his own dwelling, his goods are safe. But when someone stronger comes on him, and overcomes him, he takes from him his whole armor in which he trusted, and divides his spoils.

"He that is not with me is against me. He who doesn't gather with me scatters. The unclean spirit, when he has gone out of the man, passes through dry places, seeking rest, and finding none, he says, 'I will turn back to my house whence I came out.' When he returns, he finds it swept and put in order. Then he goes, and takes seven other spirits more evil than himself, and they enter in and dwell there. The last state of that man becomes worse than the first."

It came to pass, as he said these things, a certain woman out of the multitude lifted up her voice, and said to him, "Blessed is the womb that bore you, and the breasts which nursed you!"

But he said, **"On the contrary, blessed are those who hear the word of God, and keep it."**

Seeking a sign[16]

When the multitudes were gathering together to him, he began to say, **"This is an evil generation. It seeks after a sign. No sign will be given to it but the sign of Jonah, the prophet. For even as Jonah became a sign to the Ninevites, so will also the Son of Man be to this generation.**

"The Queen of the South will rise up in the judgment with the men of this generation, and will condemn them: for she came from the ends of the earth to hear the wisdom of Solomon; and behold, one

---

[16] Another close repetition of what He said previously

greater than Solomon is here. The men of Nineveh will stand up in the judgment with this generation, and will condemn it: for they repented at the preaching of Jonah, and behold, one greater than Jonah is here.

The lamp of the body
Source: Lk. 11:33-36

"No man, when he has lit a lamp, puts it in a cellar, nor under a basket, but on the stand, that they which enter in may see the light. The lamp of the body is the eye. Therefore when your eye is good, your whole body also is full of light; but when it is evil, your body also is full of darkness. Therefore see whether the light that is in you isn't darkness. If therefore your whole body is full of light, having no part dark, it will be wholly full of light, as when the lamp with its bright shining gives you light."

Woe to the Pharisees and lawyers
Source: Lk. 11:37-54

Now as he spoke, a certain Pharisee asked him to dine with him. He went in, and sat at the table. When the Pharisee saw it, he marveled that he had not first washed himself before dinner.

The Lord said to him, **"Now you Pharisees cleanse the outside of the cup and of the platter, but your inward part is full of extortion and wickedness. You foolish ones, didn't he who made the outside make the inside also? But give for gifts to the needy those things which are within, and behold, all things will be clean to you.**

"But woe to you Pharisees! For you tithe mint and rue and every herb, and bypass justice and the love of God. You ought to have done these, and not to have left the other undone. Woe to you Pharisees! For you love the best seats in the synagogues, and the

greetings in the marketplaces. Woe to you, scribes and Pharisees, hypocrites! For you are like hidden graves, and the men who walk over them don't know it."

One of the lawyers answered him, "Teacher, in saying this you insult us also."

He said, "Woe to you lawyers also! For you load men with burdens that are difficult to carry, and you yourselves won't even lift one finger to help carry those burdens. Woe to you! For you build the tombs of the prophets, and your fathers killed them. So you testify and consent to the works of your fathers. For they killed them, and you build their tombs.

"Therefore also the wisdom of God said, 'I will send to them prophets and apostles; and some of them they will kill and persecute, that the blood of all the prophets, which was shed from the foundation of the world, may be required of this generation; from the blood of Abel to the blood of Zachariah, who perished between the altar and the sanctuary.'

"Yes, I tell you, it will be required of this generation. Woe to you lawyers! For you took away the key of knowledge. You didn't enter in yourselves, and those who were entering in, you hindered."

As he said these things to them, the scribes and the Pharisees began to be terribly angry, and to draw many things out of him; laying in wait for him, and seeking to catch him in something he might say, that they might accuse him.

Beware of hypocrisy

Source: Lk. 12:1-34

Meanwhile, when a multitude of many thousands had gathered together, so much so that they trampled on each other, he began to tell his disciples first of all, **"Beware of the yeast of the Pharisees, which is hypocrisy. But there is nothing covered up, that will not be revealed, nor hidden, that will not be known. Therefore whatever you have said in the darkness will be heard in the light. What you have spoken in the ear in the inner chambers will be proclaimed on the housetops.**

Jesus teaches fear of God
"I tell you, my friends, don't be afraid of those who kill the body, and after that have no more that they can do. But I will warn you whom you shall fear. Fear him, who after he has killed, has power to cast into Gehenna *[Hell]*. **Yes, I tell you, fear him. Aren't five sparrows sold for two assaria** *[copper coins]*? **Not one of them is forgotten by God. But the very hairs of your head are all numbered. Therefore don't be afraid. You are of more value than many sparrows.**

Confess Christ before men
"I tell you, everyone who confesses me before men, him will the Son of Man also confess before the angels of God; but he who denies me in the presence of men will be denied in the presence of the angels of God. Everyone who speaks a word against the Son of Man will be forgiven, but those who blaspheme against the Holy Spirit will not be forgiven.

'**When they bring you before the synagogues, the rulers, and the authorities, don't be anxious how or what you will answer, or what you will say; for the Holy Spirit will teach you in that same hour what you must say."**

The parable of the rich fool

One of the multitude said to him, "Teacher, tell my brother to divide the inheritance with me."

But he said to him, "**Man, who made me a judge or an arbitrator over you?**"

He said to them, "**Beware! Keep yourselves from covetousness, for a man's life doesn't consist of the abundance of the things which he possesses.**"

He spoke a parable to them, saying, "**The ground of a certain rich man brought forth abundantly. He reasoned within himself, saying, 'What will I do, because I don't have room to store my crops?' He said, 'This is what I will do. I will pull down my barns, and build bigger ones, and there I will store all my grain and my goods. I will tell my soul, "Soul, you have many goods laid up for many years. Take your ease, eat, drink, be merry."'**

"**But God said to him, 'You foolish one, tonight your soul is required of you. The things which you have prepared — whose will they be?' So is he who lays up treasure for himself, and is not rich toward God.**"

Do not worry

He said to his disciples, "**Therefore I tell you, don't be anxious for your life, what you will eat, nor yet for your body, what you will wear. Life is more than food, and the body than clothing. Consider the ravens: they don't sow, they don't reap, they have no warehouse or barn, and God feeds them. How much more valuable are you than birds!**

"**Which of you by being anxious can add a cubit to his height? If** then you aren't able to do even the least things, why are you anxious about the rest? Consider the lilies, how they grow. They don't toil, neither do they spin; yet I tell you, even Solomon in all his glory was not arrayed like one of these. But if this is how God clothes the grass in the field, which today exists, and tomorrow is cast into the oven, how much more will he clothe you, you of little faith?

"Don't seek what you will eat or what you will drink; neither be anxious. For the nations of the world seek after all of these things, but your Father knows that you need these things. Yet seek God's kingdom, and all these things will be added to you.

Treasure in Heaven

"Don't be afraid, little flock, for it is your Father's good pleasure to give you the kingdom. Sell that which you have, and give gifts to the needy. Make for yourselves purses which don't grow old, a treasure in the heavens that doesn't fail, where no thief approaches, neither moth destroys. For where your treasure is, there will your heart be also."

~ 13 ~

Humble Will Be Exalted

This chapter includes stories of how to serve and please God and the parable of the lost sheep.

The faithful servant and the evil servant
Location: Judea and/or Perea   Source: Lk. 12:35-59

"Let your loins be girded about, and your lamps burning. Be like men looking for their lord, when he will return from the marriage feast; that, when he comes and knocks, they may immediately open to him. Blessed are those servants, whom the lord will find watching when he comes.

"Most assuredly I tell you, that he will gird himself, and make them recline, and will come and serve them. They will be blessed if he comes in the second or third watch, and finds them so. But know this, that if the master of the house had known in what hour the thief was coming, he would have watched, and not allowed his house to be broken into. Therefore be ready also, for the Son of Man is coming in an hour that you don't expect him."

Peter said to him, "Lord, are you telling this parable to us, or to everybody?"

The Lord said, "Who then is the faithful and wise steward, whom his lord will set over his household, to give them their portion of food at the right times? Blessed is that servant whom his lord will find doing so when he comes. Truly I tell you, that he will set him over all that he has.

"But if that servant says in his heart, 'My lord delays his coming,' and begins to beat the menservants and the maidservants, and to eat and drink, and to be drunken, then the lord of that servant will come in a day when he isn't expecting him, and in an hour that he doesn't know, and will cut him apart, and place his portion with the unfaithful.

"That servant, who knew his lord's will, and didn't prepare, nor do what he wanted, will be beaten with many stripes, but he who didn't know, and did things worthy of stripes, will be beaten with few stripes. To whoever much is given, of him will much be required; and to whom they deposit much, of him will they ask more.

Christ brings division

"I came to throw fire on the earth. I wish it were already kindled. But I have a baptism to be baptized with, and how distressed I am until it is accomplished! Do you think that I have come to give peace in the earth? I tell you, no, but rather division. For from now on, there will be five in one house divided, three against two, and two against three. They will be divided, father against son, and son against father; mother against daughter, and daughter against her mother; mother-in-law against her daughter-in-law, and daughter-in-law against her mother-in-law."

Discern the time

He said to the multitudes also, "When you see a cloud rising from the west, immediately you say, 'A shower is coming,' and so it happens. When a south wind blows, you say, 'There will be a scorching heat,' and it happens. You hypocrites! You know how to interpret the appearance of the earth and the sky, but how is it that you don't interpret this time?

Make peace with your adversary

"Why don't you judge for yourselves what is right? For as you are going with your adversary before the magistrate, try diligently on the way to be freed from him, lest perhaps he drag you to the judge, and the judge deliver you to the officer, and the officer throw you into prison. I tell you, you will by no means get out of there, until you have paid the very last penny."

Repent or perish

Source: Lk. 13:1-21

Now there were some present at the same time who told him about the Galilaeans, whose blood Pilate had mixed with their sacrifices.

Jesus answered them, "Do you think that these Galilaeans were worse sinners than all the other Galilaeans, because they suffered such things? I tell you, no, but, unless you repent, you will all perish in the same way. Or those eighteen, on whom the tower in Siloam fell, and killed them; do you think that they were worse offenders than all the men who dwell in Jerusalem? I tell you, no, but, unless you repent, you will all perish in the same way."

The parable of the barren fig tree

He spoke this parable. "A certain man had a fig tree planted in his vineyard, and he came seeking fruit on it, and found none. He said to the vine dresser, 'Behold, these three years I came seeking fruit on this fig tree, and found none. Cut it down. Why does it waste the soil?' He answered, 'Lord, leave it alone this year also, until I dig around it, and fertilize it. If it bears fruit, fine; but if not, after that, you can cut it down.'"

Humble Will Be Exalted

Woman healed of infirmity

He was teaching in one of the synagogues on the Sabbath day. Behold, there was a woman who had a spirit of infirmity eighteen years, and she was bent over, and could in no way straighten herself up.

When Jesus saw her, he called her, and said to her, **"Woman, you are freed from your infirmity."**

He laid his hands on her, and immediately she stood up straight, and glorified God. The ruler of the synagogue, being moved with indignation because Jesus had healed on the Sabbath, said to the multitude, "There are six days in which men ought to work. Therefore come on those days and be healed, and not on the Sabbath day!"

Therefore the Lord answered him, **"You hypocrites! Doesn't each one of you free his ox or his donkey from the stall on the Sabbath, and lead him away to water? Ought not this woman, being a daughter of Abraham, whom Satan had bound eighteen long years, be freed from this bondage on the Sabbath day?"**

As he said these things, all his adversaries were put to shame, and all the multitude rejoiced for all the glorious things that were done by him.

The parable of the mustard seed

He said, **"To what is the kingdom of God like? To what shall I compare it? It is like a grain of mustard seed, which a man took, and threw into his own garden. It grew, and became a large tree, and the birds of the sky lodged in the branches of it."**

The parable of the leaven

Again he said, **"What shall I compare to the kingdom of God? It is like yeast, which a woman took and hid in three sata** *[measures]* **of flour, until it was all leavened."**

Feast of dedication; the shepherd knows his sheep
Location: Jerusalem Source: Jn. 10:22-42

It was the Feast of the Dedication at Jerusalem. It was winter, and Jesus was walking in the temple, in Solomon's porch. The Jews therefore came around him and said to him, "How long will you hold us in suspense? If you are the Christ, tell us plainly."

Jesus answered them, **"I told you, and you don't believe. The works that I do in my Father's name, these testify about me. But you don't believe, because you are not of my sheep, as I told you. My sheep hear my voice, and I know them, and they follow me. I give eternal life to them. They will never perish, and no one will snatch them out of my hand. My Father, who has given them to me, is greater than all. No one is able to snatch them out of my Father's hand. I and the Father are one."**

Renewed efforts to stone Jesus
Therefore Jews took up stones again to stone him.

Jesus answered them, **"I have shown you many good works from my Father. For which of those works do you stone me?"**

The Jews answered him, "We don't stone you for a good work, but for blasphemy: because you, being a man, make yourself God."

Jesus answered them, **"Isn't it written in your law, 'I said, you are gods?' If he called them gods, to whom the word of God came (and the Scripture can't be broken), do you say of him whom the Father sanctified and sent into the world, 'You blaspheme,' because I said, 'I am the Son of God?' If I don't do the works of my Father, don't believe me. But if I do them, though you don't believe me, believe the works; that you may know and believe that the Father is in me, and I in the Father."**

Humble Will Be Exalted

They sought again to seize him, and he went forth out of their hand.

He went away again beyond the Jordan into the place where John was at the first baptizing, and there he stayed. Many came to him. They said, "John indeed did no sign, but everything that John said about this man is true." Many believed in him there.

The narrow way
Location: Perea to Jerusalem   *Source: Lk. 13:22-35*

He went on his way through cities and villages, teaching, and traveling on to Jerusalem. One said to him, "Lord, are they few who are saved?"

He said to them, **"Strive to enter in by the narrow door, for many, I tell you, will seek to enter in, and will not be able. When once the master of the house has risen up, and has shut the door, and you begin to stand outside, and to knock at the door, saying, 'Lord, Lord, open to us!' then he will answer and tell you, 'I don't know you or where you come from.' Then you will begin to say, 'We ate and drink in your presence, and you taught in our streets.'**

"He will say, 'I tell you, I don't know where you come from. Depart from me, all you workers of iniquity.' There will be weeping and gnashing of teeth, when you see Abraham, Isaac, Jacob, and all the prophets, in the kingdom of God, and yourselves being thrown outside. They will come from the east, west, north, and south, and will sit down in the kingdom of God. Behold, there are some who are last who will be first, and there are some who are first who will be last."

On that same day, some Pharisees came, saying to him, "Get out of here, and go away, for Herod wants to kill you."

He said to them, **"Go and tell that fox, 'Behold, I cast out demons** and perform cures today and tomorrow, and the third day I complete my mission. Nevertheless I must go on my way today and tomorrow and the next day, for it can't be that a prophet perish out of Jerusalem.'

Jesus laments over Jerusalem

"Jerusalem, Jerusalem, that kills the prophets, and stones those who are sent to her! How often I wanted to gather your children together, like a hen gathers her own brood under her wings, and you refused! Behold, your house is left to you desolate. I tell you, you will not see me, until you say, 'Blessed is he who comes in the name of the Lord!'"

A man with dropsy is healed on the Sabbath

Source: Lk. 14:1-35

It happened, when he went into the house of one of the rulers of the Pharisees on a Sabbath to eat bread, that they were watching him. Behold, a certain man who had dropsy was in front of him.

Jesus, answering, spoke to the lawyers and Pharisees, saying, **"Is it lawful to heal on the Sabbath?"**

But they were silent. He took him, and healed him, and let him go.

He answered them, **"Which of you, if your son or an ox fell into a well, wouldn't immediately pull him out on a Sabbath day?"**
They couldn't answer him regarding these things.

Take the lowly place

He spoke a parable to those who were invited, when he noticed how they chose the best seats, and said to them, **"When you are invited by anyone to a marriage feast, don't sit in the best seat, since perhaps** a more honorable man than you might be invited by him, and he who invited both of you would come and tell you, 'Make room for this man.' Then you would begin, with shame, to take the lowest place.

"But when you are invited, go and sit in the lowest place, so that when he who invited you comes, he may tell you, 'Friend, move up higher.' Then you will have glory in the presence of all who sit at the table with you. For everyone who exalts himself will be humbled, and whoever humbles himself will be exalted."

He also said to the one who had invited him, "When you make a dinner or a supper, don't call your friends, nor your brothers, nor your kinsmen, nor rich neighbors, or perhaps they might also return the favor, and pay you back. But when you make a feast, ask the poor, the maimed, the lame, or the blind; and you will be blessed, because they don't have the resources to repay you. For you will be repaid in the resurrection of the righteous."

The parable of the great supper
When one of those who sat at the table with him heard these things, he said to him, "Blessed is he who will feast in the kingdom of God!"

But he said to him, "A certain man made a great supper, and he invited many people. He sent out his servant at supper time to tell those who were invited, 'Come, for everything is ready now.' They all as one began to make excuses. The first said to him, 'I have bought a field, and I must go and see it. Please have me excused.' Another said, 'I have bought five yoke of oxen, and I must go try them out. Please have me excused.' Another said, 'I have married a wife, and therefore I can't come.' That servant came, and told his lord these things.

"Then the master of the house, being angry, said to his servant, 'Go out quickly into the streets and lanes of the city, and bring in here the poor, maimed, blind, and lame.' The servant said, 'Lord, it is done as you commanded, and there is still room.' The lord said to the servant, 'Go out into the highways and hedges, and compel them to come in, that my house may be filled. For I tell you that none of those men who were invited will taste of my supper.'"

Leaving all to follow Christ

Now great multitudes went with him. He turned and said to them, "If any man comes to me, and doesn't hate his own father, mother, wife, children, brothers, and sisters, yes, and his own life also, he can't be my disciple. Whoever doesn't bear his own cross, and come after me, can't be my disciple. For which of you, desiring to build a tower, doesn't first sit down and count the cost, to see if he has enough to complete it? Or perhaps, when he has laid a foundation, and is not able to finish, everyone who sees begins to mock him, saying, 'This man began to build, and wasn't able to finish.'

"Or what king, as he goes to encounter another king in war, will not sit down first and consider whether he is able with ten thousand to meet him who comes against him with twenty thousand? Or else, while the other is yet a great way off, he sends an envoy, and asks for conditions of peace. So therefore whoever of you who doesn't renounce all that he has, he can't be my disciple.

"Salt is good, but if the salt becomes flat and tasteless, with what do you season it? It is fit neither for the soil nor for the manure pile. It is thrown out. He who has ears to hear, let him hear."

The parable of the lost sheep

Source: Lk. 15:1-10

Now all the tax collectors and sinners were coming close to him to hear him. The Pharisees and the scribes murmured, saying, "This man welcomes sinners, and eats with them."

He told them this parable. **"Which of you men, if you had one hundred sheep, and lost one of them, wouldn't leave the ninety-nine in the wilderness, and go after the one that was lost, until he found it? When he has found it, he carries it on his shoulders, rejoicing. When he comes home, he calls together his friends and his neighbors, saying to them, 'Rejoice with me, for I have found my sheep which was lost!'** I tell you that even so there will be more joy in heaven over one sinner who repents, than over ninety-nine righteous people who need no repentance.

The parable of the lost coin
"Or what woman, if she had ten drachma [*a silver coin*] **coins, if she lost one drachma, wouldn't light a lamp, sweep the house, and seek diligently until she found it? When she has found it, she calls together her friends and neighbors, saying, 'Rejoice with me, for I have found the drachma which I had lost.'** Even so, I tell you, there is joy in the presence of the angels of God over one sinner repenting."

— 14 —

Straying Prodigal Son

This chapter starts with the famous and moving story of the prodigal son. It is a metaphor for how God loves us even in our sin and that His forgiveness and acceptance is available whenever we return to Him. Jesus also relates a story of a beggar who goes to Heaven but a rich man who does not, illustrating the irrelevance of worldly riches.

The parable of the prodigal son
Location: Perea   Source: Lk. 15:11-32

He said, "A certain man had two sons. The younger of them said to his father, 'Father, give me my share of your property.' He divided his living to them. Not many days after, the younger son gathered all of this together and took his journey into a far country. There he wasted his property with riotous living. When he had spent all of it, there arose a severe famine in that country, and he began to be in need.

"He went and joined himself to one of the citizens of that country, and he sent him into his fields to feed pigs. He wanted to fill his belly with the husks that the pigs ate, but no one gave him any. But when he came to himself he said, 'How many hired servants of my father's have bread enough to spare, and I'm dying with hunger! I will get up and go to my father, and will tell him, "Father, I have sinned against heaven, and in your sight. I am no more worthy to be called your son. Make me as one of your hired servants."'

"He arose, and came to his father. But while he was still far off, his father saw him, and was moved with compassion, and ran, and fell on his neck, and kissed him. The son said to him, 'Father, I have sinned against heaven, and in your sight. I am no more worthy to be called your son.' But the father said to his servants, 'Bring out the best robe, and put it on him. Put a ring on his hand, and shoes on his feet. Bring the fattened calf, kill it, and let us eat, and celebrate; for this, my son, was dead, and is alive again. He was lost, and is found.' They began to be merry.

"Now his elder son was in the field. As he came and drew near to the house, he heard music and dancing. He called one of the servants to him, and asked what was going on. He said to him, 'Your brother has come, and your father has killed the fattened calf, because he has received him safe and sound.' But he was angry, and would not go in. Therefore his father came out, and begged him. But he answered his father, 'Behold, these many years I served you, and I never disobeyed a commandment of yours, and you never gave me a goat, that I might celebrate with my friends. But when this, your son, came, who has devoured your living with prostitutes, you killed the fattened calf for him.'

"He said to him, 'Son, you are always with me, and all that is mine is yours. But it was appropriate to celebrate and be glad, for this, your brother, was dead, and is alive again. He was lost, and is found.' "

The parable of the unjust steward

Source: Lk. 16:1-31

He said also to his disciples, "There was a certain rich man, who had a manager. The same was accused to him of wasting his possessions. He called him, and said to him, 'What is this that I hear about you? Give an accounting of your management, for you can no longer be manager.'

"The steward said within himself, 'What will I do, seeing that my lord is taking away the management position from me? I don't have strength to dig. I am ashamed to beg. I know what I will do, so that when I am removed from management, they may receive me into their houses.'

"Calling each one of his lord's debtors to him, he said to the first, 'How much do you owe to my lord?' He said, 'A hundred batos of oil.' He said to him, 'Take your bill, and sit down quickly and write fifty.' Then said he to another, 'How much do you owe?' He said, 'A hundred cors of wheat.' He said to him, 'Take your bill, and write eighty.'

"His lord commended the unrighteous steward because he had done wisely, for the sons of this world are, in their own generation, wiser than the sons of the light. I tell you, make for yourselves friends by means of unrighteous mammon *[money or riches]*, so that when you fail, they may receive you into the eternal tents.

"He who is faithful in a very little is faithful also in much. He who is unrighteous in a very little is also unrighteous in much. If therefore you have not been faithful in the unrighteous mammon, who will commit to your trust the true riches? If you have not been faithful in that which is another's, who will give you that which is your own?

"No servant can serve two masters, for either he will hate the one, and love the other; or else he will hold to one, and despise the other. You aren't able to serve God and mammon *[money or riches]*."

The law, the prophets, and the kingdom

The Pharisees, who were lovers of money, also heard all these things, and they scoffed at him.

He said to them, "You are those who justify yourselves in the sight of men, but God knows your hearts. For that which is exalted among men is an abomination in the sight of God. The law and the prophets were until John. From that time the gospel of the kingdom of God is preached, and everyone is forcing his way into it.

"But it is easier for heaven and earth to pass away, than for one tiny stroke of a pen in the law to fall. Everyone who divorces his wife, and marries another, commits adultery. He who marries one who is put away from a husband commits adultery.

The rich man and Lazarus

"Now there was a certain rich man, and he was clothed in purple and fine linen, living in luxury every day. A certain beggar, named Lazarus, was laid at his gate, full of sores, and desiring to be fed with the crumbs that fell from the rich man's table. Yes, even the dogs came and licked his sores. It happened that the beggar died, and that he was carried away by the angels to Abraham's bosom. The rich man also died, and was buried.

"In Hades, he lifted up his eyes, being in torment, and saw Abraham far off, and Lazarus at his bosom. He cried and said, 'Father Abraham, have mercy on me, and send Lazarus, that he may dip the tip of his finger in water, and cool my tongue! For I am in anguish in this flame.'

"But Abraham said, 'Son, remember that you, in your lifetime, received your good things, and Lazarus, in like manner, bad things.

But now here he is comforted and you are in anguish. Besides all this, between us and you there is a great gulf fixed, that those who want to pass from here to you are not able, and that none may cross over from there to us.'

"He said, 'I ask you therefore, father, that you would send him to my father's house; for I have five brothers, that he may testify to them, lest they also come into this place of torment.'

"But Abraham said to him, 'They have Moses and the prophets. Let them listen to them.'

"He said, 'No, father Abraham, but if one goes to them from the dead, they will repent.'

"He said to him, 'If they don't listen to Moses and the prophets, neither will they be persuaded if one rises from the dead.'"

Jesus warns of offenses

Source: Lk. 17:1-10

He said to the disciples, "It is impossible that occasions of stumbling should not come, but woe to him through whom they come! It would be better for him if a millstone were hanged about his neck, and he were thrown into the sea, rather than that he should cause one of these little ones to stumble. Be careful. If your brother sins against you, rebuke him. If he repents, forgive him. If he sins against you seven times in the day, and seven times turns again, saying, 'I repent,' you shall forgive him."

Faith and duty

The apostles said to the Lord, "Increase our faith."

The Lord said, "If you had faith as a grain of mustard seed, you would tell this sycamore tree, 'Be uprooted, and be planted in the sea,' and it would obey you. But who is there of you, having a servant plowing or keeping sheep, that will say, when he comes in from the field, 'Come immediately and sit down at the table,' and will not rather tell him, 'Prepare my supper, clothe yourself properly, and serve me, while I eat and drink. Afterward you will eat and drink?'

"Does he thank that servant because he did the things that were commanded? I think not. Even so you also, when you have done all the things that are commanded you, say, 'We are unworthy servants. We have done our duty.'"

— 15 —

I am Resurrection and Life

Jesus starkly proclaims, "I am the resurrection and the life. He who believes in me, though he die, yet will he live." He raises Lazarus from the dead. And He describes "the coming of the Kingdom" events that will occur upon His second coming. He repeats His assertion that whomever is humbled will be exalted.

Death of Lazarus

Location: Perea to Bethany   *Source: Jn. 11:1-57*

Now a certain man was sick, Lazarus of Bethany, of the village of Mary and her sister, Martha. It was that Mary who anointed the Lord with ointment, and wiped his feet with her hair,[17] whose brother, Lazarus, was sick. The sisters therefore sent to him, saying, "Lord, behold, he for whom you have great affection is sick."

But when Jesus heard it, he said, **"This sickness is not to death, but for the glory of God, that God's Son may be glorified by it."**

---

[17] Clarification: This statement in John's gospel can be confusing because the anointing of Jesus by Mary has not yet happened! Indeed, John does not report it until later in his gospel. Writing well after all these events, he mentions it here only to clarify which Mary he means, believing that her (subsequent) anointing of Jesus is already well known (about Mary and the anointing, Jesus said, "wherever this gospel will be preached in the whole world, what this woman has done will also be spoken of for a memorial of her").

I Am Resurrection and Life

Now Jesus loved Martha, and her sister, and Lazarus. When therefore he heard that he was sick, he stayed at that time two days in the place where he was. Then after this he said to the disciples, **"Let's go into Judea again."**

The disciples told him, "Rabbi, the Jews were just trying to stone you, and are you going there again?"

Jesus answered, **"Aren't there twelve hours of daylight? If a man walks in the day, he doesn't stumble, because he sees the light of this world. But if a man walks in the night, he stumbles, because the light isn't in him."**

He said these things, and after that, he said to them, **"Our friend, Lazarus, has fallen asleep, but I am going so that I may awake him out of sleep."**

The disciples therefore said to him, "Lord, if he has fallen asleep, he will recover." Now Jesus had spoken of his death, but they thought that he spoke of taking rest in sleep.

So Jesus said to them plainly then, **"Lazarus is dead. I am glad for your sakes that I was not there, so that you may believe. Nevertheless, let's go to him."**

Thomas therefore, who is called Didymus, said to his fellow disciples, "Let's go also, that we may die with him."

Jesus is the resurrection and the life
So when Jesus came, he found that he had been in the tomb four days already. Now Bethany was near Jerusalem, about fifteen stadia away. Many of the Jews had come to Martha and Mary, to console them concerning their brother. Therefore Martha, when she heard that

Jesus was coming, went and met him, but Mary stayed in the house. Therefore Martha said to Jesus, "Lord, if you would have been here, my brother wouldn't have died. Even now I know that, whatever you ask of God, God will give you."

Jesus said to her, **"Your brother will rise again."**

Martha said to him, "I know that he will rise again in the resurrection at the last day."

Jesus said to her, **"I am the resurrection and the life. He who believes in me, though he die, yet will he live. Whoever lives and believes in me will never die. Do you believe this?"**

She said to him, "Yes, Lord. I have come to believe that you are the Christ, God's Son, he who comes into the world."

When she had said this, she went away, and called Mary, her sister, secretly, saying, "The Teacher is here, and is calling you." She, when she heard this, arose quickly, and went to him. Now Jesus had not yet come into the village, but was in the place where Martha met him. Then the Jews who were with her in the house, and were consoling her, when they saw Mary, that she rose up quickly and went out, followed her, saying, "She is going to the tomb to weep there."

Mary therefore, when she came to where Jesus was, and saw him, fell down at his feet, saying to him, "Lord, if you would have been here, my brother wouldn't have died."

When Jesus therefore saw her weeping, and the Jews weeping who came with her, he groaned in the spirit, and was troubled, and said, **"Where have you laid him?"**

I Am Resurrection and Life

They told him, "Lord, come and see." Jesus wept. The Jews therefore said, "See how much affection he had for him!" Some of them said, "Couldn't this man, who opened the eyes of him who was blind, have also caused that this man wouldn't die?"

Lazarus raised from the dead

Jesus therefore, again groaning in himself, came to the tomb. Now it was a cave, and a stone lay against it. Jesus said, **"Take away the stone."**

Martha, the sister of him who was dead, said to him, "Lord, by this time there is a stench, for he has been dead four days."

Jesus said to her, **"Didn't I tell you that if you believed, you would see God's glory?"**

So they took away the stone from the place where the dead man was lying.

Jesus lifted up his eyes, and said, **"Father, I thank you that you listened to me. I know that you always listen to me, but because of the multitude that stands around I said this, that they may believe that you sent me."**

When he had said this, he cried with a loud voice, **"Lazarus, come out!"**

He who was dead came out, bound hand and foot with wrappings, and his face was wrapped around with a cloth. Jesus said to them, **"Free him, and let him go."**

[Although the rest of John 11 (verses 45-57) contains no words of Jesus, it is included here because it summarizes the decision to kill

Jesus. It illustrates the danger he would walk into when next he returned to Jerusalem.]

Therefore many of the Jews, who came to Mary and saw that which Jesus did, believed in him. But some of them went away to the Pharisees, and told them the things which Jesus had done. The chief priests therefore and the Pharisees gathered a council, and said, "What are we doing? For this man does many signs. If we leave him alone like this, everyone will believe in him, and the Romans will come and take away both our place and our nation."

But a certain one of them, Caiaphas, being high priest that year, said to them, "You know nothing at all, nor do you take account that it is advantageous for us that one man should die for the people, and that the whole nation not perish." Now he didn't say this of himself, but being high priest that year, he prophesied that Jesus would die for the nation, and not for the nation only, but that he might also gather together into one the children of God who are scattered abroad. So from that day forth they took counsel that they might put him to death.

Jesus therefore walked no more openly among the Jews, but departed from there into the country near the wilderness, into a city called Ephraim. He stayed there with his disciples. Now the Passover of the Jews was at hand. Many went up to Jerusalem out of the country before the Passover, to purify themselves. Then they sought for Jesus and spoke one with another, as they stood in the temple, "What do you think? Isn't he coming to the feast?" Now the chief priests and the Pharisees had commanded that if anyone knew where he was, he should report it, that they might seize him.

Ten lepers cleansed
Location: Going to Jerusalem via Samaria & Galilee   Source: Lk. 17:11-37

It happened, as he was on his way to Jerusalem, that he was passing along the borders of Samaria and Galilee. As he entered into a certain village, ten men who were lepers met him, who stood far away. They lifted up their voices, saying, "Jesus, Master, have mercy on us!"

When he saw them, he said to them, **"Go and show yourselves to the priests."**

It happened, as they went, they were cleansed. One of them, when he saw that he was healed, turned back, glorifying God with a loud voice. He fell on his face at his feet, giving him thanks. He was a Samaritan.

Jesus answered, **"Weren't the ten cleansed? But where are the nine? Were there none found who returned to give glory to God, except this stranger?"**

He said to him, **"Get up, and go your way. Your faith has healed you."**

The coming of the Kingdom

Being asked by the Pharisees when the kingdom of God would come, he answered them, **"The kingdom of God doesn't come with observation; neither will they say, 'Look, here!' or, 'Look, there!' for behold, the kingdom of God is within you."**

He said to the disciples, **"The days will come, when you will desire to see one of the days of the Son of Man, and you will not see it. They will tell you, 'Look, here!' or 'Look, there!' Don't go away, nor follow after them, for as the lightning, when it flashes out of the one part under the sky, shines to the other part under the sky; so will the Son of Man be in his day. But first, he must suffer many things and be rejected by this generation.**

"As it happened in the days of Noah, even so will it be also in the days of the Son of Man. They ate, they drank, they married, they were given in marriage, until the day that Noah entered into the ark, and the flood came, and destroyed them all. Likewise, even as it happened in the days of Lot: they ate, they drank, they bought, they sold, they planted, they built; but in the day that Lot went out from Sodom, it rained fire and sulfur from the sky, and destroyed them all.

"It will be the same way in the day that the Son of Man is revealed. In that day, he who will be on the housetop, and his goods in the house, let him not go down to take them away. Let him who is in the field likewise not turn back. Remember Lot's wife! Whoever seeks to gain his life loses it, but whoever loses his life preserves it.

"I tell you, in that night there will be two people in one bed. The one will be taken, and the other will be left. There will be two women grinding together. The one will be taken, and the other will be left."

They answering, asked him, "Where, Lord?"

He said to them, "**Where the body is, there will the vultures also be gathered together.**"

The parable of the persistent widow

Source: Lk. 18:1-14

He also spoke a parable to them that they must always pray, and not give up, saying, "**A certain judge was in a city, who didn't fear God, and didn't respect man. A widow was in that city, and she came often to him, saying, 'Defend me from my adversary!' He wouldn't for a while, but afterward he said to himself, 'Though I don't fear

God, nor respect man, yet because this widow bothers me, I will defend her, or else she will wear me out by her continual coming.'"

The Lord said, "Listen to what the unrighteous judge says. Won't God avenge his elect, who are crying out to him day and night, and yet he exercises patience with them? I tell you that he will avenge them quickly. Nevertheless, when the Son of Man comes, will he find faith on the earth?"

The parable of the Pharisee and the tax collector

He spoke also this parable to certain people who were convinced of their own righteousness, and who despised all others. "Two men went up into the temple to pray; one was a Pharisee, and the other was a tax collector. The Pharisee stood and prayed to himself like this: 'God, I thank you, that I am not like the rest of men, extortioners, unrighteous, adulterers, or even like this tax collector. I fast twice in the week. I give tithes of all that I get.'

"But the tax collector, standing far away, wouldn't even lift up his eyes to heaven, but beat his breast, saying, 'God, be merciful to me, a sinner!' I tell you, this man went down to his house justified rather than the other; for everyone who exalts himself will be humbled, but he who humbles himself will be exalted."

Marriage and divorce

Location: Judea/Perea   *Source: Mt. 19:1-7; Mk. 10:3-4;*
Mt. 19:8-9; Mk. 10:12; Mt. 19:10-12

It happened when Jesus had finished these words, he departed from Galilee, and came into the borders of Judea beyond the Jordan. Great multitudes followed him, and he healed them there. Pharisees came to him, testing him, and saying, "Is it lawful for a man to divorce his wife for any reason?"

He answered, "Haven't you read that he who made them from the beginning made them male and female, and said, 'For this cause a man will leave his father and mother, and will join to his wife; and the two will become one flesh?' So that they are no more two, but one flesh. What therefore God has joined together, don't let man tear apart."

They asked him, "Why then did Moses command us to give her a bill of divorce, and divorce her?"

He answered, **"What did Moses command you?"**

They said, "Moses allowed a bill of divorce to be written, and to divorce her."

But Jesus said to them, **"For your hardness of heart, he wrote you this commandment."**

He said to them, **"Moses, because of the hardness of your hearts, allowed you to divorce your wives, but from the beginning it has not been so. I tell you that whoever will put away his wife, except for sexual immorality, and will marry another, commits adultery; and he who marries her when she is put away commits adultery. If a woman herself divorces her husband, and marries another, she commits adultery."**

His disciples said to him, "If this is the case of the man with his wife, it is not expedient to marry."

Celibacy

But he said to them, **"Not all men can receive this saying, but they to whom it is given. For there are eunuchs, who were born that way from their mother's womb, and there are eunuchs, who were made** eunuchs by men: and there are eunuchs who made themselves eunuchs for the Kingdom of Heaven's sake. He who is able to receive it, let him receive it."

~ 16 ~

All Things Are Possible; Jesus Is Anointed

Jesus again addresses the false belief in that time that riches were a sign of God's favor and blessing. He proclaims that a trust in riches is baseless. He proclaims that with God all things are possible. Mary anoints Jesus.

Jesus blesses little children

Location: Perea   Source: Mk. 10:13-16

They were bringing to him little children, that he should touch them, but the disciples rebuked those who were bringing them.

But when Jesus saw it, he was moved with indignation, and said to them, **"Allow the little children to come to me! Don't forbid them, for to such belong the kingdom of God. Most assuredly I tell you, whoever will not receive the kingdom of God as a little child, he will in no way enter therein."**

He took them in his arms, and blessed them, laying his hands on them.

Jesus counsels the rich young ruler
Source: Mk. 10:17; Mt. 19:17-18; Mk. 10:19;
Mt. 19:19-20; Mk. 10:21-22 (+Mt. 19:21)

As he was going forth into the way, one *["a certain ruler" according*

All Things Are Possible; Jesus Is Anointed

to Luke] ran to him, kneeled to him, and asked him, "Good Teacher, what shall I do that I may inherit eternal life?"

He said to him, **"Why do you call me good? No one is good but one, that is, God. But if you want to enter into life, keep the commandments."**

He said to him, "Which ones?"

Jesus said, **"You know the commandments: 'Do not murder,' 'Do not commit adultery,' 'Do not steal,' 'Do not give false testimony,' 'Do not defraud,' 'Honor your father and mother.' And, 'you shall love your neighbor as yourself.'"**

The young man said to him, "All these things I have observed from my youth. What do I still lack?"

Jesus looking at him loved him, and said to him, **"One thing you lack. If you want to be perfect, go, sell what you have, and give to the poor, and you will have treasure in heaven; and come, follow me, taking up the cross."**

But his face fell at that saying, and he went away sorrowful, for he was one who had great possessions.

With God all things are possible
Source: Lk. 18:24; Mk. 10:24-27; Mt. 19:27-28; Mk. 10:29-31

Jesus, seeing that he became very sad, said, **"How hard it is for those who have riches to enter into the kingdom of God!"**

The disciples were amazed at his words.[18]

---

[18] Many in those days viewed riches as evidence of approval and blessing from God.

But Jesus answered again, "Children, how hard is it for those who trust in riches to enter into the kingdom of God! It is easier for a camel to go through a needle's eye than for a rich man to enter into the kingdom of God."

They were exceedingly astonished, saying to him, "Then who can be saved?"

Jesus, looking at them, said, **"With men it is impossible, but not with God, for all things are possible with God."**

Then Peter answered, "Behold, we have left everything, and followed you. What then will we have?"

Jesus said to them, **"Most assuredly I tell you, that you who have followed me, in the regeneration when the Son of Man will sit on the throne of his glory, you also will sit on twelve thrones, judging the twelve tribes of Israel."**

Jesus said, **"Most assuredly I tell you, there is no one who has left house, or brothers, or sisters, or father, or mother, or wife, or children, or land, for my sake, and for the gospel's sake, but he will receive one hundred times now in this time, houses, brothers, sisters, mothers, children, and land, with persecutions; and in the age to come eternal life. But many who are first will be last; and the last first."**

The parable of the workers in the Vineyard

Source: Mt. 20:1-16

"For the Kingdom of Heaven is like a man who was the master of a household, who went out early in the morning to hire laborers for his vineyard. When he had agreed with the laborers for a denarius a day, he sent them into his vineyard. He went out about the third

hour *[9 am]*, and saw others standing idle in the marketplace. To them he said, 'You also go into the vineyard, and whatever is right I will give you.' So they went their way.

"Again he went out about the sixth *[noon]* and the ninth *[3 pm]* hour, and did likewise. About the eleventh hour *[5 pm]* he went out, and found others standing idle. He said to them, 'Why do you stand here all day idle?' They said to him, 'Because no one has hired us.' He said to them, 'You also go into the vineyard, and you will receive whatever is right.'

"When evening had come, the lord of the vineyard said to his steward, 'Call the laborers and pay them their hire, beginning from the last to the first.' When they who were hired at about the eleventh hour came, they each received a denarius. When the first came, they supposed that they would receive more; and they likewise each received a denarius. When they received it, they murmured against the master of the household, saying, 'These last have spent one hour, and you have made them equal to us, who have borne the burden of the day and the scorching heat!'

"But he answered one of them, 'Friend, I am doing you no wrong. Didn't you agree with me for a denarius? Take that which is yours, and go your way. It is my will to give to this last just as much as to you. Isn't it lawful for me to do what I want to with what I own? Or is your eye evil, because I am good?'

"So the last will be first, and the first last. For many are called, but few are chosen."

Jesus predicts his death and resurrection a third time
Location: Near Jordan   Source: Mk. 10:32; Lk. 18:31; Mt. 20:18-19 (+Lk. 18:32); Lk. 18:34

They were on the way, going up to Jerusalem; and Jesus was going in front of them, and they were amazed; and those who followed were afraid. He again took the twelve, and began to tell them the things that were going to happen to him.

"Behold, we are going up to Jerusalem, and all the things that are written through the prophets concerning the Son of Man will be completed. The Son of Man will be delivered to the chief priests and scribes, and they will condemn him to death, and will hand him over to the Gentiles to mock, to scourge, *[to be]* treated shamefully, and spit on, and to crucify; and the third day he will be raised up."

They understood none of these things. This saying was hidden from them, and they didn't understand the things that were said.

Ambition of James and John (Greatness is in serving)
Source: Mk. 10:35-37; Mt. 20:22-28

James and John, the sons of Zebedee, came near to him, saying, "Teacher, we want you to do for us whatever we will ask."

He said to them, **"What do you want me to do for you?"**

They said to him, "Grant to us that we may sit, one at your right hand, and one at your left hand, in your glory."[19]

But Jesus answered, **"You don't know what you ask. Are you able to drink the cup that I am about to drink, and be baptized with the baptism that I am baptized with?"**

---

[19] Matthew records that the mother of James and John also requested this or joined in the request.

All Things Are Possible; Jesus Is Anointed

They said to him, "We are able."

He said to them, **"You will indeed drink my cup, and be baptized with the baptism that I am baptized with, but to sit on my right hand, and on my left hand, is not mine to give; but it is for whom it has been prepared by my Father."**

When the ten heard it, they were moved with indignation concerning the two brothers.

But Jesus called them to him, and said, **"You know that the rulers of the Gentiles lord it over them, and their great ones exercise authority over them. It shall not be so among you, but whoever would become great among you will be your servant. Whoever would be first among you will be your bondservant, even as the Son of Man came not to be served, but to serve, and to give his life as a ransom for many."**

Blind Bartimaeus healed[20]

Location: Jericho   *Source: Mk. 10:46-51; Lk. 18:42-43 (+Mt. 10:52)*

They came to Jericho. As he went out from Jericho, with his disciples and a great multitude, the son of Timaeus, Bartimaeus, a blind beggar, was sitting by the road. When he heard that it was Jesus, the Nazarene, he began to cry out, and say, "Jesus, you son of David, have mercy on me!" Many rebuked him, that he should be quiet, but he cried out the more a great deal, "You son of David, have mercy on me!"

Jesus stood still, and said, **"Call him."**

They called the blind man, saying to him, "Cheer up! Get up. He is calling you." He, casting away his cloak, sprang up, and came to Jesus.

---

[20] Matthew records that two blind men were healed. Only one of the two is reported by Mark and Luke.

Jesus answered him, **"What do you want me to do for you?"**

The blind man said to him, "Rhabboni, that I may see again."

Jesus said to him, **"Receive your sight. Go your way. Your faith has healed you."**

Immediately he received his sight, and followed him, glorifying God. All the people, when they saw it, praised God.

Jesus comes to the house of Zacchaeus

Source: Lk. 19:1-27

He *[Jesus]* entered and was passing through Jericho. There was a man named Zacchaeus. He was a chief tax collector, and he was rich. He was trying to see who Jesus was, and couldn't because of the crowd, because he was short. He ran on ahead, and climbed up into a sycamore tree to see him, for he was to pass that way.

When Jesus came to the place, he looked up and saw him, and said to him, **"Zacchaeus, hurry and come down, for today I must stay at your house."**

He hurried, came down, and received him joyfully. When they saw it, they all murmured, saying, "He has gone in to lodge with a man who is a sinner." Zacchaeus stood and said to the Lord, "Behold, Lord, half of my goods I give to the poor. If I have wrongfully exacted anything of anyone, I restore four times as much."

Jesus said to him, **"Today, salvation has come to this house, because he also is a son of Abraham. For the Son of Man came to seek and to save that which was lost."**

The parable of the Minas [units of currency]

As they heard these things, he went on and told a parable, because he was near Jerusalem, and they supposed that the kingdom of God would be revealed immediately.

He said therefore, "A certain nobleman went into a far country to receive for himself a kingdom, and to return. He called ten servants of his, and gave them ten minas, and told them, 'Conduct business until I come.' But his citizens hated him, and sent an envoy after him, saying, 'We don't want this man to reign over us.'

"It happened, when he had come back again, having received the kingdom, that he commanded these servants, to whom he had given the money, to be called to him, that he might know what they had gained by conducting business.

"The first came before him, saying, 'Lord, your mina has made ten more minas.' He said to him, 'Well done, you good servant! Because you were found faithful in a very little, you shall have authority over ten cities.' The second came, saying, 'Your mina, Lord, has made five minas.' He said to him also, 'You also are to be over five cities.' Another came, saying, 'Lord, behold, your mina, which I kept laid away in a handkerchief, for I feared you, because you are an exacting man. You take up that which you didn't lay down, and reap that which you didn't sow.'

"He said to him, 'Out of your own mouth will I judge you, you wicked servant! You knew that I am an exacting man, taking up that which I didn't lay down, and reaping that which I didn't sow. Then why didn't you deposit my money in the bank, and I at my coming might have earned interest on it?' He said to those who stood by, 'Take the mina away from him, and give it to him who has the ten minas.' They said to him, 'Lord, he has ten minas!'

"For I tell you that to everyone who has, will more be given; but from him who doesn't have, even that which he has will be taken away from him. But bring those enemies of mine who didn't want me to reign over them here, and kill them before me."

Anointing by Mary at Simon's house

Location: At Bethany, near Jerusalem   Source: Jn. 12:1-2; Mk. 14:3-5; Jn. 12:3-6; Mk. 14:6-9

[Note: there is debate among Bible historians whether this anointing was one event or two similar events. See Appendix for discussion.]

Six days before the Passover, Jesus came to Bethany, where Lazarus was, who had been dead, whom he raised from the dead. So they made him a supper there. Martha served, but Lazarus was one of those who sat at the table with him.

While he was at Bethany, in the house of Simon the leper, as he sat at the table, there came a woman *[Mary]* having an alabaster jar of ointment of pure nard *[oil of spikenard]* — very costly. She broke the jar, and poured it over his head. But there were some who had indignation among themselves, saying, "Why has this ointment been wasted? For this might have been sold for more than three hundred denarii, and given to the poor." They grumbled against her.

Mary, therefore, took a pound of ointment of pure nard, very precious, and anointed the feet of Jesus, and wiped his feet with her hair. The house was filled with the fragrance of the ointment. Then Judas Iscariot, Simon's son, one of his disciples, who would betray him, said, "Why wasn't this ointment sold for three hundred denarii, and given to the poor?" Now he said this, not because he cared for the poor, but because he was a thief, and having the money box, used to steal what was put into it.

All Things Are Possible; Jesus Is Anointed

But Jesus said, "**Leave her alone. Why do you trouble her?** She has done a good work for me. For you always have the poor with you, and whenever you want to, you can do them good; but you will not always have me. She has done what she could. She has anointed my body beforehand for the burying. Most assuredly I tell you, wherever this gospel may be preached throughout the whole world, that also which this woman has done will be spoken of for a memorial of her."

~ 17 ~

Final Week; Triumphal Entry

The final week of Jesus' life on earth begins with His famous triumphal entry into Jerusalem. Christians celebrate that day as "Palm Sunday," one week before Easter. Also herein is Jesus' emphasis on the need to forgive others for God to forgive you. All events during this week took place in or just outside of Jerusalem.

Triumphal Entry into Jerusalem

Location: Bethany & Jerusalem   Source: Mt. 21:1-8 (+Mk. 11:2); Mk. 11:9-10; Lk. 19:39-44; Mk. 11:11

When they drew near to Jerusalem, and came to Bethsphage, to the Mount of Olives, then Jesus sent two disciples, saying to them, **"Go into the village that is opposite you, and immediately you will find a donkey tied, and a colt with her, on which no one has sat. Untie them, and bring them to me. If anyone says anything to you, you will say, 'The Lord needs them,' and immediately he will send them."**

All this was done, that it might be fulfilled which was spoken through the prophet, saying,

> "Tell the daughter of Zion,
> Behold, your King comes to you,
> Humble, and riding on a donkey,
> On a colt, the foal of a donkey."[21]

---

[21] Zechariah 9:9

Final Week; Triumphal Entry

The disciples went, and did just as Jesus commanded them, and brought the donkey and the colt, and laid their clothes on them; and he sat on them. A very great multitude spread their clothes on the road. Others cut branches from the trees, and spread them on the road. Those who went in front, and those who followed, cried,

"Hosanna!
Blessed is he who comes in the name of the Lord!
Blessed is the kingdom of our father David that is coming in the name of the Lord! Hosanna in the highest!"

Some of the Pharisees from the multitude said to him, "Teacher, rebuke your disciples!"

He answered them, **"I tell you that if these were silent, the stones would cry out."**

Jesus weeps over Jerusalem

When he drew near, he saw the city and wept over it, saying, **"If you, even you, had known today the things which belong to your peace! But now, they are hidden from your eyes. For the days will come on you, when your enemies will throw up a barricade against you, surround you, hem you in on every side, and will dash you and your children within you to the ground. They will not leave in you one stone on another, because you didn't know the time of your visitation."**

Jesus entered into the temple in Jerusalem. When he had looked around at everything, it being now evening, he went out to Bethany with the twelve.

Jesus curses a fig tree

Source: Mk. 11:12-14

The next day, when they had come out from Bethany, he was hungry. Seeing a fig tree afar off having leaves, he came to see if perhaps he might find anything on it. When he came to it, he found nothing but leaves, for it was not the season for figs.

Jesus told it, **"May no one ever eat fruit from you again!"** and his disciples heard it.

Second cleansing of the Temple

Source: Mk. 11:15-17; Mt. 21:14-17

They came to Jerusalem, and Jesus entered into the temple, and began to throw out those who sold and those who bought in the temple, and overthrew the tables of the money-changers, and the seats of those who sold the doves. He would not allow anyone to carry a container through the temple.

He taught, saying to them, **"Isn't it written, 'My house will be called a house of prayer for all the nations?' But you have made it a 'den of robbers!'"**[22]

The blind and the lame came to him in the temple, and he healed them. But when the chief priests and the scribes saw the wonderful things that he did, and the children who were crying in the temple and saying, "Hosanna to the son of David!" they were moved with indignation, and said to him, "Do you hear what these are saying?"

Jesus said to them, **"Yes. Did you never read, 'Out of the mouth of babes and nursing babies you have perfected praise?'"**[23]

---

[22] Isaiah 56:7 and Jeremiah 7:11
[23] Psalm 8:2

Final Week; Triumphal Entry

He left them, and went forth out of the city to Bethany, and lodged there.

The lesson of the withered fig tree
Source: Mk. 11:20-21; Mt. 21:20-21; Mk. 11:22-26

As they passed by in the morning, they saw the fig tree withered away from the roots. Peter, remembering, said to him, "Rabbi, look! The fig tree which you cursed has withered away." When the disciples saw it, they marveled, saying, "How did the fig tree immediately wither away?"

Jesus answered them, **"Most assuredly I tell you, if you have faith, and don't doubt, you will not only do what is done to the fig tree, but even if you will tell this mountain, 'Be taken up and cast into the sea,' it will be done.**

"Have faith in God. For most assuredly I tell you, whoever may tell this mountain, 'Be taken up and cast into the sea,' and doesn't doubt in his heart, but believes that what he says happens; he shall have whatever he says. Therefore I tell you, all things whatever you pray and ask for, believe that you receive them, and you shall have them.

Forgiveness and prayer
"Whenever you stand praying, forgive, if you have anything against anyone; so that your Father, who is in heaven, may also forgive you your transgressions. But if you do not forgive, neither will your Father in heaven forgive your transgressions."

Jesus' authority questioned
Source: Mk. 11:27-28; Mt. 21:24-27

They came again to Jerusalem, and as he was walking in the temple, the chief priests, and the scribes, and the elders came to him, and they began saying to him, "By what authority do you these things? Or who gave you this authority to do these things?"

Jesus answered them, **"I also will ask you one question, which if you tell me, I likewise will tell you by what authority I do these things. The baptism of John, where was it from? From heaven or from men?"**

They reasoned with themselves, saying, "If we will say, 'From heaven,' he will tell us, 'Why then did you not believe him?' But if we will say, 'From men,' we fear the multitude, for all hold John as a prophet." They answered Jesus, and said, "We don't know."

He also said to them, **"Neither will I tell you by what authority I do these things.**

The parable of the two sons

Source: Mt. 21:28-46

"But what do you think? A man had two sons, and he came to the first, and said, 'Son, go work today in my vineyard.' He answered, 'I will not,' but afterward he repented himself, and went. He came to the second, and said likewise. He answered, 'I go, sir,' but he didn't go. Which of the two did the will of his father?"

They said to him, "The first."

Jesus says to them, **"Most assuredly I tell you, that the tax collectors and the prostitutes are entering into the kingdom of God before you. For John came to you in the way of righteousness, and you didn't believe him, but the tax collectors and the prostitutes believed him. When you saw it, you didn't even repent afterward, that you might believe him.**

The parable of the wicked vinedressers

"Hear another parable. There was a man who was a master of a household, who planted a vineyard, set a hedge about it, dug a winepress in it, built a tower, leased it out to farmers, and went into another country. When the season of the fruits drew near, he sent his servants to the farmers, to receive his fruits. The farmers took his servants, beat one, killed another, and stoned another. Again, he sent other servants more than the first: and they did to them in like manner.

"But afterward he sent to them his son, saying, 'They will respect my son.' But the farmers, when they saw the son, said among themselves, 'This is the heir. Come, let's kill him, and seize his inheritance.' So they took him, and threw him out of the vineyard, and killed him. When therefore the lord of the vineyard will come, what will he do to those farmers?"

They told him, "He will miserably destroy those miserable men, and will lease out the vineyard to other farmers, who will give him the fruits in their seasons."

Jesus said to them, "**Did you never read in the Scriptures,**

> 'The stone which the builders rejected,
> The same was made the head of the corner.
> This was from the Lord.
> It is marvelous in our eyes?'[24]

"Therefore I tell you, the kingdom of God will be taken away from you, and will be given to a nation bringing forth its fruits. He who falls on this stone will be broken to pieces, but on whoever it will fall, it will scatter him as dust."

---

[24] Psalm 118:22,23

When the chief priests and the Pharisees heard his parables, they perceived that he spoke of them. When they sought to lay hold on him, they feared the multitudes, because they took him for a prophet.

The parable of the wedding feast

Source: Mt. 22:1-14

Jesus answered and spoke again in parables to them, saying, "**The Kingdom of Heaven is like a certain king, who made a marriage feast for his son, and sent forth his servants to call those who were invited to the marriage feast, but they would not come. Again he sent forth other servants, saying, 'Tell those who are invited, "Behold, I have made ready my dinner. My oxen and my fatlings are killed, and all things are ready. Come to the marriage feast."'**

"But they made light of it, and went their ways, one to his own farm, another to his merchandise, and the rest grabbed his servants, and treated them shamefully, and killed them. But the king was angry, and he sent his armies, destroyed those murderers, and burned their city. Then he said to his servants, 'The wedding is ready, but they who were invited were not worthy. Go therefore to the intersections of the highways, and as many as you may find, invite to the marriage feast.'

"Those servants went out into the highways, and gathered together as many as they found, both bad and good. The wedding was filled with guests. But when the king came in to see the guests, he saw there a man who didn't have on wedding-clothing, and he said to him, 'Friend, how did you come in here not having wedding-clothing?' He was speechless. Then the king said to the servants, 'Bind him hand and foot, take him away, and throw him into the outer darkness; there is where the weeping and grinding of teeth will be.'

"For many are called, but few chosen."

Final Week; Triumphal Entry

Pharisees and taxes to Caesar
Source: Mt. 22:15; Lk. 20:20-22; Mt. 22:18-22

Then the Pharisees went and took counsel how they might entrap him in his talk. They watched him, and sent out spies, who pretended to be righteous, that they might trap him in something he said, so as to deliver him up to the rule and to the authority of the governor. They asked him, "Teacher, we know that you say and teach what is right, and aren't partial to anyone, but truly teach the way of God. Is it lawful for us to pay taxes to Caesar, or not?"

But Jesus perceived their wickedness, and said, **"Why do you test me, you hypocrites? Show me the tax money."**

They brought to him a denarius.

He asked them, **"Whose is this image and inscription?"**

They said to him, "Caesar's."

Then he said to them, **"Give therefore to Caesar the things that are Caesar's, and to God the things that are God's."**

When they heard it, they marveled, and left him, and went away.

Sadducees question the resurrection
Source: Mk. 12:18-23; Lk. 20:34-36; Mk. 12:24-27; Lk. 20:39-40

There came to him Sadducees, who say that there is no resurrection. They asked him, saying, "Teacher, Moses wrote to us, 'If a man's brother dies, and leaves a wife behind him, and leaves no children, that his brother should take his wife, and raise up offspring for his brother.' There were seven brothers. The first took a wife, and dying left no offspring. The second took her, and died, leaving no children behind him. The third likewise; and the seven took her and left no children. Last of all the woman also died. In the resurrection, when they rise, whose wife will she be of them? For the seven had her as a wife."

Jesus said to them, **"The sons of this age marry, and are given in marriage. But those who are considered worthy to attain to that age and the resurrection from the dead, neither marry, nor are given in marriage. For neither can they die any more, for they are like the angels, and are sons of God, being sons of the resurrection."**

Jesus answered them, **"Isn't this because you are mistaken, not knowing the Scriptures, nor the power of God? For when they will rise from the dead, they neither marry, nor are given in marriage, but are like angels in heaven. But about the dead, that they are raised; haven't you read in the book of Moses, at the Bush, how God spoke to him, saying, 'I am the God of Abraham, the God of Isaac, and the God of Jacob?' He is not the God of the dead, but of the living. You are therefore badly mistaken."**

Some of the scribes answered, "Teacher, you speak well." They didn't dare to ask him any more questions.

~ 18 ~

Greatest Commandment

Jesus famously gives the two greatest commandments, to love God and to love your neighbor. He criticizes those who make show of their religious devotion for public approval. Also herein is His famous story of the widow's "two mites" and the huge value of her seemingly tiny gift.

The Pharisees ask which is the first commandment of all
Location: Jerusalem   *Source: Mt. 22:34-36; Mk. 12:29-30;*
Mt. 22:38-40; Mk. 12:31-34

But the Pharisees, when they heard that he had put the Sadducees to silence, gathered themselves together. One of them, a lawyer, asked him a question, testing him. "Teacher, which is the greatest commandment in the law?"

Jesus answered, **"The greatest is, 'Hear, Israel, the Lord our God, the Lord is one: you shall love the Lord your God with all your heart, and with all your soul, and with all your mind, and with all your strength.' This is the first and great commandment. A second likewise is this, 'You shall love your neighbor as yourself.' The whole law and the prophets depend on these two commandments. There is no other commandment greater than these."**

The scribe said to him, "Truly, teacher, you have said well that he is one, and there is none other but he, and to love him with all the heart, and with all the understanding, with all the soul, and with all the strength, and to love his neighbor as himself, is more than all whole burnt offerings and sacrifices."

When Jesus saw that he answered wisely, he said to him, **"You are not far from the kingdom of God."**

No one dared ask him any question after that.

Whose son is Christ?
Source: Mt. 22:41-42; Mk. 12:35-36; Mt. 22:45-46

Now while the Pharisees were gathered together, Jesus asked them a question, saying, **"What do you think of the Christ? Whose son is he?"**

They said to him, "Of David."

Jesus responded, as he taught in the temple, **"How is it that the scribes say that the Christ is the son of David? For David himself said in the Holy Spirit,**

> **'The Lord said to my Lord,**
> **Sit at my right hand,**
> **Until I make your enemies the footstool of your feet.'**[25]

"If then David calls him Lord, how is he his son?"

No one was able to answer him a word, neither dared any man from that day forth ask him any more questions.

---

[25] Psalm 110:1

Greatest Commandment

Woe to the Scribes and Pharisees; pride condemned
Source: Mk. 12:38-40; Mt. 23:1-39

In his teaching he said to them, "**Beware of the scribes, who desire to walk in long robes, and to get greetings in the marketplaces, and chief seats in the synagogues, and chief places at feasts: those who devour widows' houses, and for a pretense make long prayers. These will receive greater condemnation.**"

Then Jesus spoke to the multitudes and to his disciples, saying, "**The scribes and the Pharisees sat on Moses' seat. All things therefore whatever they tell you to observe, observe and do, but don't do their works; for they say, and don't do. For they bind heavy burdens that are grievous to be borne, and lay them on men's shoulders; but they themselves will not lift a finger to help them.**

"**But all their works they do to be seen by men. They make their phylacteries broad, enlarge the fringes of their garments, and love the chief place at feasts, the chief seats in the synagogues, the salutations in the marketplaces, and to be called 'Rabbi, Rabbi' by men. But don't you be called 'Rabbi,' for one is your teacher, the Christ, and all of you are brothers. Call no man on the earth your father, for one is your Father, he who is in heaven. Neither be called masters, for one is your master, the Christ.**

"**But he who is greatest among you will be your servant. Whoever will exalt himself will be humbled, and whoever will humble himself will be exalted.**

"**Woe to you, scribes and Pharisees, hypocrites! For you devour widows' houses, and as a pretense you make long prayers. Therefore you will receive greater condemnation. But woe to you, scribes and Pharisees, hypocrites! Because you shut up the Kingdom of Heaven against men; for you don't enter in yourselves,** neither do you allow those who are entering in to enter. Woe to you, scribes and Pharisees, hypocrites! For you travel around by sea and land to make one proselyte; and when he becomes one, you make him twice as much of a son of Gehenna *[Hell]* as yourselves.

"Woe to you, you blind guides, who say, 'Whoever swears by the temple, it is nothing; but whoever swears by the gold of the temple, he is a debtor.' You blind fools! For which is greater, the gold, or the temple that sanctifies the gold? 'Whoever will swear by the altar, it is nothing; but whoever will swear by the gift that is on it, he is a debtor.' You blind fools! For which is greater, the gift, or the altar that sanctifies the gift.

"He therefore who swears by the altar, swears by it, and by everything on it. He who swears by the temple, swears by it, and by him who is living in it. He who swears by the heaven, swears by the throne of God, and by him who sits on it.

"Woe to you, scribes and Pharisees, hypocrites! For you tithe mint, dill, and cumin, and have left undone the weightier matters of the law - justice, mercy, and faith. But you ought to have done these, and not to have left the other undone. You blind guides, who strain out a gnat, and swallow a camel!

"Woe to you, scribes and Pharisees, hypocrites! For you clean the outside of the cup and of the platter, but within they are full of extortion and unrighteousness. You blind Pharisee, first clean the inside of the cup and of the platter, that the outside of it may become clean also.

"Woe to you, scribes and Pharisees, hypocrites! For you are like whitened tombs, which outwardly appear beautiful, but inwardly are full of dead men's bones, and of all uncleanness. Even so you also outwardly appear righteous to men, but inwardly you are full of hypocrisy and iniquity.

"Woe to you, scribes and Pharisees, hypocrites! For you build the tombs of the prophets, and decorate the tombs of the righteous, and say, 'If we had been in the days of our fathers, we should not have been partakers with them in the blood of the prophets.'

"Therefore you testify to yourselves that you are sons of those who killed the prophets. Fill up, then, the measure of your fathers. You serpents, you offspring of vipers, how will you escape the judgment of Gehenna [hell]? Therefore, behold, I send to you prophets, wise men, and scribes. Some of them will you kill and crucify; and some of them will you scourge in your synagogues, and persecute from city to city; that on you may come all the righteous blood shed on the earth, from the blood of Abel the righteous to the blood of Zachariah son of Barachiah, whom you killed between the sanctuary and the altar. Most assuredly I tell you, all these things will come on this generation.

Jesus laments over Jerusalem

"Jerusalem, Jerusalem, that kills the prophets, and stones those who are sent to her! How often would I have gathered your children together, even as a hen gathers her chickens under her wings, and you would not! Behold, your house is left to you desolate. For I tell you, you will not see me from now on, until you will say, 'Blessed is he who comes in the name of the Lord.'"

The widow's two mites

Source: Mk. 12:41-44

Jesus sat down opposite the treasury, and saw how the multitude cast money into the treasury. Many who were rich cast in much. A poor widow came, and she cast in two lepta *[some translations say "two mites"[26], which make a quadrans.*

He called his disciples to himself, and said to them, **"Most assuredly I tell you, this poor widow gave more than all those who are giving into the treasury, for they all gave out of their abundance, but she, out of her poverty, gave all that she had to live on."**

---

[26] The lepton was the lowest value coin. Many traditional biblical translations say "mite" to emphasize its minimum value. Hence, the well known phrase, "the widow's two mites."

— 19 —

Great Tribulation Coming

Jesus predicts future events, including the end of the age where there will be great tribulation and Jesus will come again to the earth (the second coming).

Jesus predicts the destruction of the Temple
Location: Jerusalem   Source: Mk. 13:1-2

As he went forth out of the temple, one of his disciples said to him, "Teacher, see what kind of stones and what kind of buildings!"

Jesus said to him, **"Do you see these great buildings? There will not be left here one stone on another, which will not be thrown down."** [27]

Jesus warns of troubling times and persecution
Source: Mk. 13:3-4; Mt. 24:4-8 (+Lk21:8); Mk. 13:9-11; Lk. 21:14-15; Mk. 13:12; Lk. 21:18-19; Mt. 24:9-14

As he sat on the Mount of Olives opposite the temple, Peter, James, John, and Andrew asked him privately, "Tell us, when will these things be? What is the sign that these things are all about to be accomplished?"

---

[27] In 70 AD a Roman army of approximately 30,000 captured Jerusalem and destroyed both the city and the Temple.

Jesus answered them, "Be careful that no one leads you astray. For many will come in my name, saying, 'I am the Christ,' and will lead many astray. Therefore don't follow them. You will hear of wars and rumors of wars. See that you aren't troubled, for all this must happen, but the end is not yet. For nation will rise against nation, and kingdom against kingdom; and there will be famines, plagues, and earthquakes in various places. But all these things are the beginning of birth pains.

"But watch yourselves, for they will deliver you up to councils. You will be beaten in synagogues. Before governors and kings will you stand for my sake, for a testimony to them. The gospel must first be preached to all the nations. When they lead you away and deliver you up, don't be anxious beforehand, or premeditate what you will say, but say whatever will be given you in that hour. For it is not you who speak, but the Holy Spirit.

"Settle it therefore in your hearts not to meditate beforehand how to answer, for I will give you a mouth and wisdom which all your adversaries will not be able to withstand or to contradict.

"Brother will deliver up brother to death, and the father his child. Children will rise up against parents, and cause them to be put to death. Not a hair of your head will perish. By your endurance you will win your lives. Then they will deliver you up to oppression, and will kill you. You will be hated by all of the nations for my name's sake.

"Then will many stumble, and will deliver up one another, and will hate one another. Many false prophets will arise, and will lead many astray. Because iniquity will be multiplied, the love of many will grow cold. But he who endures to the end, the same will be saved. This gospel of the kingdom will be preached in the whole world for a testimony to all the nations, and then the end will come.

The destruction of Jerusalem
Source: Lk. 21:20-24

"But when you see Jerusalem surrounded by armies, then know that its desolation is at hand. Then let those who are in Judea flee to the mountains. Let them who are in the midst of her depart. Don't let those who are in the country enter therein. For these are days of vengeance, that all things which are written may be fulfilled.

"Woe to those who are pregnant and to those who nurse infants in those days! For there will be great distress in the land, and wrath to this people. They will fall by the edge of the sword, and will be led captive into all the nations. Jerusalem will be trampled down by the Gentiles, until the times of the Gentiles are fulfilled.

The great tribulation, false Christs and prophets
Source: Mt. 24:15-16; Mk. 13:15-17; Mt. 24:20; Mk. 13:19-23; Mt. 24:26-28

"When, therefore, you see the abomination of desolation, which was spoken of through Daniel the prophet, standing in the holy place (let the reader understand), then let those who are in Judea flee to the mountains.

"And let him who is on the housetop not go down, nor enter in, to take anything out of his house. Let him who is in the field not return back to take his cloak. But woe to those who are with child and to those who nurse babies in those days! Pray that your flight will not be in the winter, nor on a Sabbath,

"For in those days there will be oppression, such as there has not been the like from the beginning of the creation which God created until now, and never will be. Unless the Lord had shortened the days, no flesh would have been saved; but for the elect's sake, whom he chose, he shortened the days. Then if anyone tells you, 'Look, here is the Christ!' or, 'Look, there!' don't believe it. For there will arise false christs and false prophets, and will show signs and wonders, that they may lead astray, if possible, also the elect. But you watch. Behold, I have told you all things beforehand.

"If therefore they tell you, 'Behold, he is in the wilderness!' don't go out; 'Behold, he is in the inner chambers,' don't believe it. For as the lightning comes forth from the east, and is seen even to the west, so will be the coming of the Son of Man. For wherever the carcass is, there will the vultures be gathered together.

The coming of the Son of Man (the second coming)
Source: Mt. 24:29; Lk. 21:25-27;
Mt. 24:30-31 (+Mk. 13:27); Lk. 21:28

"But immediately after the oppression of those days, the sun will be darkened, the moon will not give her light, the stars will fall from the sky, and the powers of the heavens will be shaken.

"There will be signs in the sun, moon, and stars; and on the earth anxiety of nations, in perplexity for the roaring of the sea and the waves; men fainting for fear, and for expectation of the things which are coming on the world: for the powers of the heavens will be shaken. Then they will see the Son of Man coming in a cloud with power and great glory.

"And then the sign of the Son of Man will appear in the sky. Then all the tribes of the earth will mourn, and they will see the Son of

Man coming on the clouds of the sky with power and great glory. He will send forth his angels with a great sound of a trumpet, and they will gather together his elect from the four winds, from the ends of the earth to the ends of the sky.

"But when these things begin to happen, look up, and lift up your heads, because your redemption is near.

The parable of the fig tree
Source: Mt. 24:32-35 (+Lk. 21:31)

"Now from the fig tree learn her parable. When its branch has now become tender, and puts forth its leaves, you know that the summer is near. Even so you also, when you see these things happening, know that the kingdom of God is near, even at the doors. Most assuredly I tell you, this generation will not pass away, until all these things are accomplished. Heaven and earth will pass away, but my words will not pass away.

No one knows the day or hour—be watchful
Source: Mk. 13:32-37; Lk. 21:34-36; Mt. 24:37-51

"But of that day or that hour no one knows, not even the angels in heaven, neither the Son, but only the Father. Watch, keep alert, and pray; for you don't know when the time is. It is like a man, traveling to another country, having left his house, and given authority to his servants, and to each one his work, and also commanded the doorkeeper to keep watch. Watch therefore, for you don't know when the lord of the house is coming, whether at evening, or at midnight, or when the rooster crows, or in the morning; lest coming suddenly he might find you sleeping. What I tell you, I tell all: Watch.

"So be careful, or your hearts will be loaded down with carousing, drunkenness, and cares of this life, and that day will come on you suddenly. For it will come like a snare on all those who dwell on the surface of all the earth. Therefore be watchful all the time, asking that you may be counted worthy to escape all these things that will happen, and to stand before the Son of Man.

"As the days of Noah, so will be the coming of the Son of Man. For as in those days which were before the flood they were eating and drinking, marrying and giving in marriage, until the day that Noah entered into the ark, and they didn't know until the flood came, and took them all away, so will be the coming of the Son of Man. Then will two men be in the field: one is taken, and one is left; two women grinding at the mill, one is taken, and one is left.

"Watch therefore, for you don't know in what hour your Lord comes. But know this, that if the master of the house had known in what watch the thief was coming, he would have watched, and would not have allowed his house to be broken into. Therefore also be ready, for in an hour that you don't expect, the Son of Man will come.

The faithful servant and the evil servant[28]
"Who then is the faithful and wise servant, whom his lord has set over his household, to give them their food in due season? Blessed is that servant, whom his lord will find doing so when he comes. Most assuredly I tell you, that he will set him over all that he has. But if that evil servant should say in his heart, 'My lord is delaying his coming,' and began to beat his fellow-servants, and eat and drink with the drunken, the lord of that servant will come in a day when he doesn't expect it, and in an hour when he doesn't know it, and will cut him in pieces, and appoint his portion with

---

[28] This is another case where Jesus tells the same parable twice, as this is almost the same as a previous passage (as reported in Lk. 12:41-48).

the hypocrites; there is where the weeping and grinding of teeth will be.

The parable of the wise and foolish virgins
Source: Mt. 25:1-46

"Then the Kingdom of Heaven will be like ten virgins, who took their lamps, and went forth to meet the bridegroom. Five of them were foolish, and five were wise. Those who were foolish, when they took their lamps, took no oil with them, but the wise took oil in their vessels with their lamps. Now while the bridegroom delayed, they all slumbered and slept.

"But at midnight there was a cry, 'Behold! The bridegroom is coming! Come out to meet him!' Then all those virgins arose, and trimmed their lamps. The foolish said to the wise, 'Give us some of your oil, for our lamps are going out.' But the wise answered, saying, 'What if there will not be enough for us and you? You go rather to those who sell, and buy for yourselves.' While they went away to buy, the bridegroom came, and those who were ready went in with him to the marriage feast, and the door was shut.

"Afterward the other virgins also came, saying, 'Lord, Lord, open to us.' But he answered, 'Most assuredly I tell you, I don't know you.' Watch therefore, for you don't know the day nor the hour in which the Son of Man is coming.

The parable of the talents[29]

"For it is like a man, going into another country, who called his own servants, and delivered his goods to them. To one he gave five talents, to another two, to another one; to each according to his

---

[29] Another case where Jesus teaches almost the same parable twice. See "The parable of the Minas," Lk. 19:11-27.

own ability, and he went on his journey. Immediately he who received the five talents went and traded with them, and made another five talents. In like manner he also who got the two gained another two. But he who received the one went away and dug in the earth, and hid his lord's money. Now after a long time the lord of those servants came, and reconciled accounts with them.

"He who received the five talents came and brought another five talents, saying, 'Lord, you delivered to me five talents. Behold, I have gained another five talents besides them.' His lord said to him, 'Well done, good and faithful servant. You have been faithful over a few things, I will set you over many things. Enter into the joy of your lord.' He also who got the two talents came and said, 'Lord, you delivered to me two talents. Behold, I have gained another two talents besides them.' His lord said to him, 'Well done, good and faithful servant. You have been faithful over a few things, I will set you over many things. Enter into the joy of your lord.'

"He also who had received the one talent came and said, 'Lord, I knew you that you are a hard man, reaping where you did not sow, and gathering where you did not scatter. I was afraid, and went away and hid your talent in the earth. Behold, you have your own.'

"But his lord answered him, 'You wicked and slothful servant. You knew that I reap where I didn't sow, and gather where I didn't scatter. You ought therefore to have deposited my money with the bankers, and at my coming I should have received back my own with interest. Take away therefore the talent from him, and give it to him who has the ten talents.

'For to everyone who has will be given, and he will have abundance, but from him who has not, even that which he has will be taken away. Throw out the unprofitable servant into the outer darkness; there will be the weeping and the gnashing of teeth.'

The Son of Man will judge the nations

"But when the Son of Man comes in his glory, and all the holy angels with him, then will he sit on the throne of his glory. Before him all the nations will be gathered, and he will separate them one from another, as the shepherd separates the sheep from the goats. He will set the sheep on his right hand, but the goats on the left. Then the King will tell them on his right hand, 'Come, blessed of my Father, inherit the kingdom prepared for you from the foundation of the world; for I was hungry, and you gave me food to eat; I was thirsty, and you gave me drink; I was a stranger, and you took me in; naked, and you clothed me; I was sick, and you visited me; I was in prison, and you came to me.'

"Then the righteous will answer him, saying, 'Lord, when did we see you hungry, and feed you; or thirsty, and give you a drink? When did we see you as a stranger, and take you in; or naked, and clothe you? When did we see you sick, or in prison, and come to you?' The King will answer them, 'Most assuredly I tell you, inasmuch as you did it to one of the least of these my brothers, you did it to me.'

"Then will he say also to them on the left hand, 'Depart from me, you cursed, into the eternal fire which is prepared for the devil and his angels; for I was hungry, and you didn't give me food to eat; I was thirsty, and you gave me no drink; I was a stranger, and you didn't take me in; naked, and you didn't clothe me; sick, and in prison, and you didn't visit me.'

"Then will they also answer, saying, 'Lord, when did we see you hungry, or thirsty, or a stranger, or naked, or sick, or in prison, and did not help you?' Then will he answer them, saying, 'Most assuredly I tell you, inasmuch as you didn't do it to one of these least, you didn't do it to me.' These will go away into eternal punishment, but the righteous into eternal life."

~ 20 ~

Public Ministry Completed

Jesus completes His public ministry. He again predicts His crucifixion. Judas agrees to betray Jesus.

The fruitful grain of wheat (final public appeal to unbelievers)

Location: Jerusalem   Source: Jn. 12:20-50

Now there were certain Greeks among those that went up to worship at the feast. These, therefore, came to Philip, who was from Bethsaida of Galilee, and asked him, saying, "Sir, we want to see Jesus." Philip came and told Andrew, and in turn, Andrew came with Philip, and they told Jesus.

Jesus answered them, **"The time has come for the Son of Man to be glorified. Most assuredly I tell you, unless a grain of wheat falls into the earth and dies, it remains by itself alone. But if it dies, it bears much fruit. He who loves his life will lose it. He who hates his life in this world will keep it to eternal life. If anyone serves me, let him follow me. Where I am, there will my servant also be. If anyone serves me, the Father will honor him.**

Jesus predicts his death

"Now my soul is troubled. What shall I say? 'Father, save me from this time?' But for this cause I came to this time. Father, glorify your name!"

Then there came a voice out of the sky, saying, "I have both glorified it, and will glorify it again." The multitude therefore, who stood by and heard it, said that it had thundered. Others said, "An angel has spoken to him."

Jesus answered, **"This voice hasn't come for my sake, but for your sakes. Now is the judgment of this world. Now the prince of this world will be cast out. I, if I am lifted up from the earth, will draw all men to myself."**

But he said this, signifying by what kind of death he should die.

The multitude answered him, "We have heard out of the law that the Christ remains forever. How do you say, 'The Son of Man must be lifted up?' Who is this Son of Man?"

Jesus therefore said to them, **"Yet a little while the light is with you. Walk while you have the light, that darkness doesn't overtake you. He who walks in the darkness doesn't know where he is going. While you have the light, believe in the light, that you may become sons of light."**

Jesus said these things, and he departed and hid himself from them. But though he had done so many signs before them, yet they didn't believe in him, that the word of Isaiah the prophet might be fulfilled, which he spoke,

> "Lord, who has believed our report?
> To whom has the arm of the Lord been revealed?"[30]

For this cause they couldn't believe, for Isaiah said again,

---

[30] Isaiah 53:1

"He has blinded their eyes and he hardened their heart,
Lest they should see with their eyes,
And perceive with their heart,
And would turn,
And I would heal them."[31]

Isaiah said these things when he saw his glory, and he spoke of him.

Walk in the light

Nevertheless even of the rulers many believed in him, but because of the Pharisees they didn't confess it, so that they wouldn't be put out of the synagogue, for they loved men's approval more than God's approval.[32]

Jesus cried out and said, **"Whoever believes in me, believes not in me, but in him who sent me. He who sees me sees him who sent me. I have come as a light into the world, that whoever believes in me may not remain in the darkness. If anyone listens to my sayings, and doesn't believe, I don't judge him. For I came not to judge the world, but to save the world.**

"He who rejects me, and doesn't receive my sayings, has one who judges him. The word that I spoke, the same will judge him in the last day. For I spoke not from myself, but the Father who sent me, he gave me a commandment, what I should say, and what I should speak. I know that his commandment is eternal life. The things therefore which I speak, even as the Father has said to me, so I speak."

---

[31] Isaiah 6:10

[32] Author's note: For me, this verse (Jn. 12:43), "for they loved men's approval more than God's approval" is one of the most chilling verses in the Bible. How often we do this, and how foolish we are!

Jesus predicts His crucifixion

Source: Mt. 26:1-5

It happened, when Jesus had finished all these words, that he said to his disciples, **"You know that after two days the Passover is coming, and the Son of Man will be delivered up to be crucified."**

Then the chief priests, the scribes, and the elders of the people were gathered together in the court of the high priest, who was called Caiaphas. They took counsel together that they might take Jesus by deceit, and kill him. But they said, "Not during the feast, lest a riot occur among the people."

Judas agrees to betray Jesus

Source: Mt. 26:14-16

Then one of the twelve, who was called Judas Iscariot,[33] went to the chief priests, and said, "What are you willing to give me, and I will deliver him to you?" They weighed out for him thirty pieces of silver. From that time he sought opportunity to betray him.

---

[33] Luke 22:3 notes that "Satan entered into Judas."

～ 21 ～

Last Gathering; Passover

Jesus meets with His disciples to celebrate Passover. This will be their last gathering. He demonstrates servanthood by washing His disciples' feet. He identifies Judas as the one who will betray Him. He gives a famous new commandment—that His followers should love one another as He loves us.

Preparation for Passover with His disciples
Location: Jerusalem　　　　　　　Source: Mk. 14:12; Lk. 22:8-13;
　　　　　　　　　　　　　　　　　　　　Mk. 14:17; Lk. 22:14-16

On the first day of unleavened bread, when they sacrificed the Passover *[lamb]*, his disciples asked him, "Where do you want us to go and make ready that you may eat the Passover?"

He sent Peter and John, saying, **"Go and prepare the Passover for us, that we may eat."**

They said to him, "Where do you want us to prepare?"

He said to them, **"Behold, when you have entered into the city, a man carrying a pitcher of water will meet you. Follow him into the house which he enters. Tell the master of the house, 'The Teacher says to you, "Where is the guest room, where I may eat the Passover with my disciples?"' He will show you a large, furnished upper room. Make preparations there."**

They went, found things as he had told them, and they prepared the Passover. When it was evening he came with the twelve.

When the hour had come, he sat down with the twelve apostles. He said to them, **"I have earnestly desired to eat this Passover with you before I suffer, for I tell you, I will no longer by any means eat of it until it is fulfilled in the kingdom of God."**

Jesus washes the disciples' feet

Source: Jn. 13:3-20

Jesus, knowing that the Father had given all things into his hands, and that he came forth from God, and was going to God, arose from supper, and laid aside his outer garments. He took a towel, and wrapped a towel around his waist.

Then he poured water into the basin, and began to wash the disciples' feet, and to wipe them with the towel that was wrapped around him. Then he came to Simon Peter. He said to him, "Lord, do you wash my feet?"[34]

Jesus answered him, **"You don't know what I am doing now, but you will understand later."**

Peter said to him, "You will never wash my feet!"

Jesus answered him, **"If I don't wash you, you have no part with me."**

Simon Peter said to him, "Lord, not my feet only, but also my hands and my head!"

---

[34] The washing of feet was considered a menial task, done only by the lowest servant. Jesus is giving an example of the servanthood He expects all His followers to emulate.

Last Gathering; Passover

Jesus said to him, "**Someone who has bathed only needs to have their feet washed, but is completely clean. You are clean, but not all of you.**"

For he knew him who would betray him, therefore he said, "**You are not all clean.**"

So when he had washed their feet, put his outer garment back on, and sat down again, he said to them, "**Do you know what I have done to you? You call me, 'Teacher' and 'Lord.' You say so correctly, for so I am. If I then, the Lord and the Teacher, have washed your feet, you also ought to wash one another's feet. For I have given you an example, that you also should do as I have done to you. Most assuredly I tell you, a servant is not greater than his lord, neither one who is sent greater than he who sent him. If you know these things, blessed are you if you do them.**

"**I don't speak concerning all of you. I know whom I have chosen. But that the Scripture may be fulfilled, 'He who eats bread with me has lifted up his heel against me.' From now on, I tell you before it happens, that when it happens, you may believe that I AM. Most assuredly I tell you, he who receives whoever I send, receives me; and he who receives me, receives him who sent me.**"

Jesus identifies His betrayer
Source: Mk. 14:18; Lk. 22:21; Mt. 26:22; Mk. 14:20-21; Mt. 26:25; Jn. 13:23-30

As they sat and were eating, Jesus said, "**Most assuredly I tell you, one of you will betray me — he who eats with me. Behold, the hand of him who betrays me is with me on the table.**"

They were exceedingly sorrowful, and each began to ask him, "It isn't me, is it, Lord?"

He answered them, **"It is one of the twelve, he who dips with me in the dish. For the Son of Man goes, even as it is written about him, but woe to that man through whom the Son of Man is betrayed! It would be better for that man if he had not been born."**

Judas, who betrayed him, answered, "It isn't me, is it, Rabbi?"

He said to him, **"So you have said."**

One of his disciples, whom Jesus loved *[John]*, was at the table, leaning against Jesus' breast. Simon Peter therefore beckoned to him, and said to him, "Tell us who it is of whom he speaks." He, leaning back, as he was, on Jesus' breast, asked him, "Lord, who is it?"

Jesus therefore answered, **"It is he to whom I will give this morsel when I have dipped it."**

So when he had dipped the morsel, he gave it to Judas, the son of Simon Iscariot. After the morsel, then Satan entered into him.

Jesus therefore said to him, **"What you do, do quickly."**

Now no man at the table knew why he said this to him. For some thought, because Judas had the money box, that Jesus said to him, "Buy what things we need for the feast," or that he should give something to the poor. Therefore, having received that morsel, he went out immediately. It was night.

Jesus gives a new Commandment—love one another

Source: Jn. 13:31-35

When he had gone out, Jesus said, **"Now the Son of Man is glorified, and God is glorified in him. If God is glorified in him, God will also glorify him in himself, and he will glorify him immediately. Little**

Last Gathering; Passover

children, yet a little while I am with you. You will seek me, and as I said to the Jews, 'Where I am going, you can't come,' so now I tell you.

"A new commandment I give to you, that you love one another, just like I have loved you; that you also love one another. By this everyone will know that you are my disciples, if you have love for one another."

~ 22 ~

The Lord's Supper

As the Passover meal continues, Jesus begins the portion that has come to be called "the Lord's Supper." He reveals many important truths, including, "I am the way, the truth, and the life. No one comes to the Father but by me." He promises the help of the Holy Spirit. He proclaims He has overcome the world. And He prays for Himself, His disciples, and all believers to come.

Jesus institutes the Lord's Supper

Location: Jerusalem *Source: Mt. 26:26; Lk. 22:19; Mt. 26:27-29 (+Lk. 22:17)*

As they were eating, Jesus took bread, gave thanks for it, and broke it. He gave to the disciples, and said, **"Take, eat; this is my body which is given for you. Do this in memory of me."**

He took the cup, gave thanks, and gave to them, saying, **"Take this, and share it among yourselves. Drink all of it, for this is my blood of the new covenant, which is poured out for many for the remission of sins. But I tell you that I will not drink of this fruit of the vine from now on, until that day when I drink it anew with you in my Father's kingdom."**

The disciples argue who is the greatest

Source: Lk. 22:24-30

There arose also a contention among them, which of them was considered to be greatest.

He said to them, **"The kings of the Gentiles lord it over them, and those who have authority over them are called 'benefactors.' But not so with you. But one who is the greater among you, let him become as the younger, and one who is governing, as one who serves.**

"For who is greater, one who sits at the table, or one who serves? Isn't it he who sits at the table? But I am in the midst of you as one who serves. But you are those who have continued with me in my temptations. I appoint to you a kingdom, even as my Father appointed to me, that you may eat and drink at my table in my kingdom. You will sit on thrones, judging the twelve tribes of Israel."

Jesus predicts they will deny him, including Peter
Source: Mt. 26:31-32; Jn. 13:36-38; Lk. 22:31-34; Mt. 26:33; Mk. 14:30-31

Then Jesus said to them, **"All of you will be offended by me tonight, for it is written,**

> **'I will strike the shepherd,**
> **and the sheep of the flock will be scattered abroad.'**[35]

But after I am raised up, I will go before you into Galilee."

Simon Peter said to him, "Lord, where are you going?"

Jesus answered, **"Where I am going, you can't follow now, but you will follow afterwards."**

Peter said to him, "Lord, why can't I follow you even now? I will lay down my life for you."

---

[35] Zechariah 13:7

Jesus answered him, "**Will you lay down your life for me? Most assuredly I tell you, the rooster won't crow until you have denied me three times.**"

The Lord said, "**Simon, Simon, behold, Satan asked to have you, that he might sift you as wheat, but I prayed for you, that your faith wouldn't fail. You, when once you have turned again, establish your brothers.**"

He said to him, "Lord, I am ready to go with you both to prison and to death!"

He said, "**I tell you, Peter, the rooster will by no means crow today, before you deny that you know me three times.**"

But Peter answered him, "Even if all will be offended by you, I will never be offended."

Jesus said to him, "**Most assuredly I tell you, that you today, even this night, before the cock crows twice, you will deny me three times.**"

But he spoke all the more, "If I must die with you, I will not deny you." Likewise, they all said so.

"I am the way, the truth, and the life"

Source: Jn. 14:1-31

"**Don't let your heart be troubled. Believe in God. Believe also in me. In my Father's house are many mansions. If it weren't so, I would have told you. I am going to prepare a place for you. If I go and prepare a place for you, I will come again, and will receive you to myself; that where I am, you may be there also. Where I go, you know, and you know the way.**"

The Lord's Supper

Thomas says to him, "Lord, we don't know where you are going. How can we know the way?"

Jesus said to him, **"I am the way, the truth, and the life. No one comes to the Father, but by me.**

The Father is revealed in Jesus
"If you had known me, you would have known my Father also. From now on, you know him, and have seen him."

Philip said to him, "Lord, show us the Father, and that will be enough for us."

Jesus said to him, **"Have I been with you such a long time, and do you not know me, Philip? He who has seen me has seen the Father. How do you say, 'Show us the Father?' Don't you believe that I am in the Father, and the Father in me? The words that I tell you, I speak not from myself; but the Father living in me does his works. Believe me that I am in the Father, and the Father in me; or else believe me for the very works' sake.**

Prayer is answered
"Most assuredly I tell you, he who believes in me, the works that I do, he will do also; and greater works than these will he do; because I am going to my Father. Whatever you will ask in my name, that will I do, that the Father may be glorified in the Son. If you will ask anything in my name, that will I do.

Jesus promises another Counselor, the Holy Spirit
"If you love me, keep my commandments. I will pray to the Father, and he will give you another Counselor, that he may be with you forever, — the Spirit of truth, whom the world can't receive; for it doesn't see him, neither knows him. You know him, for he lives

with you, and will be in you. I will not leave you orphans. I will come to you.

Indwelling of the Father and the Son

"Yet a little while, and the world will see me no more; but you will see me. Because I live, you will live also. In that day you will know that I am in my Father, and you in me, and I in you. Someone who has my commandments, and keeps them, that person is one who loves me. One who loves me will be loved by my Father, and I will love him, and will reveal myself to him."

Judas (not Iscariot) said to him, "Lord, what will happen that you will reveal yourself to us, and not to the world?"

Jesus answered him, "If a man loves me, he will keep my word. My Father will love him, and we will come to him, and make our home with him. He who doesn't love me doesn't keep my words. The word which you hear isn't mine, but the Father's who sent me.

The gift of peace

"I have said these things to you, while still living with you. But the Counselor, the Holy Spirit, whom the Father will send in my name, he will teach you all things, and bring to your memory all that I said to you. Peace I leave with you. My peace I give to you; not as the world gives, give I to you. Don't let your heart be troubled, neither let it be fearful.

"You heard how I told you, 'I go away, and I come to you.' If you loved me, you would have rejoiced, because I said 'I am going to my Father;' for the Father is greater than I. Now I have told you before it happens so that, when it happens, you may believe. I will no more speak much with you, for the prince of the world comes, and he has nothing in me. But that the world may know that I love the Father, and as the Father commanded me, even so I do. Arise, let us go from here."

Jesus warns them to be prepared
Source: Lk. 22:35-39

He said to them, "When I sent you out without purse, and wallet, and shoes, did you lack anything?"

They said, "Nothing."

Then he said to them, "But now, whoever has a purse, let him take it, and likewise a wallet. Whoever has none, let him sell his cloak, and buy a sword. For I tell you that this which is written must still be fulfilled in me: 'He was counted with the lawless.' For that which concerns me has an end."

They said, "Lord, behold, here are two swords."

He said to them, "**That is enough.**"

He came out, and went, as his custom was, to the Mount of Olives. His disciples also followed him.

Jesus is the true vine
Source: Jn. 15:1-27, 16:1-33

"I am the true vine, and my Father is the farmer. Every branch in me that doesn't bear fruit, he takes away. Every branch that bears fruit, he prunes, that it may bear more fruit. You are already pruned clean because of the word which I have spoken to you. Remain in me, and I in you. As the branch can't bear fruit by itself, unless it remains in the vine, so neither can you, unless you remain in me.

"I am the vine. You are the branches. He who remains in me, and I in him, the same bears much fruit, for apart from me you can do nothing. If a man doesn't remain in me, he is thrown out as a branch, and is withered; and they gather them, throw them into the fire, and they are burned. If you remain in me, and my words remain in you, you will ask whatever you desire, and it will be done to you. In this is my Father glorified, that you bear much fruit; and so you will be my disciples.

Love and joy perfected

"Even as the Father has loved me, I also have loved you. Remain in my love. If you keep my commandments, you will remain in my love; even as I have kept my Father's commandments, and remain in his love. I have spoken these things to you, that my joy may be in you, and that your joy may be made full. This is my commandment, that you love one another, even as I have loved you. Greater love has no one than this, that a man lay down his life for his friends.

"You are my friends, if you do whatever I command you. No longer do I call you servants, for the servant doesn't know what his lord does. But I have called you friends, for everything that I heard from my Father, I have made known to you. You didn't choose me, but I chose you, and appointed you, that you should go and bear fruit, and that your fruit should remain; that whatever you will ask of the Father in my name, he may give it to you. I command these things to you, that you may love one another.

The world's hatred

"If the world hates you, you know that it has hated me before it hated you. If you were of the world, the world would love its own. But because you are not of the world, since I chose you out of the world, therefore the world hates you. Remember the word that I said to you: 'A servant is not greater than his lord.' If they persecuted me, they will also persecute you. If they kept my word, they will keep yours also.

"But all these things will they do to you for my name's sake, because they don't know him who sent me. If I had not come and spoken to them, they would not have had sin; but now they have no excuse for their sin. He who hates me, hates my Father also. If I hadn't done among them the works which no one else did, they wouldn't have had sin. But now have they seen and also hated both me and my Father. But that the word may be fulfilled that is written in their law, 'They hated me without a cause.'

The coming rejection

"When the Counselor has come, whom I will send to you from the Father, the Spirit of truth, who proceeds from the Father, he will testify about me. You will also testify, because you have been with me from the beginning.

"These things have I spoken to you, so that you wouldn't be caused to stumble. They will put you out of the synagogues. Yes, the time comes that whoever kills you will think that he offers service to God. They will do these things because they have not known the Father, nor me. But I have told you these things, so that when the time comes, you may remember that I told you about them. I didn't tell you these things from the beginning, because I was with you.

The work of the Holy Spirit

"But now I am going to him who sent me, and none of you asks me, 'Where are you going?' But because I have told you these things, sorrow has filled your heart. Nevertheless I tell you the truth: It is to your advantage that I go away, for if I don't go away, the

Counselor won't come to you. But if I go, I will send him to you. When he has come, he will convict the world in respect to sin, and righteousness, and judgment; of sin, because they don't believe in me; of righteousness, because I am going to my Father, and you see me no more; of judgment, because the prince of this world has been judged.

"I have yet many things to tell you, but you can't bear them now. However when he, the Spirit of truth, has come, he will guide you into all the truth, for he will not speak from himself; but whatever things he hears, he will speak. He will declare to you the things that are to come. He will glorify me, for he will take from what is mine, and will declare it to you. All things whatever the Father has are mine; therefore I said that he takes of mine, and will declare it to you.

Sorrow will turn to joy

"A little while, and you will not see me. Again a little while, and you will see me."

Some of his disciples therefore said to one another, "What is this that he says to us, 'A little while, and you won't see me, and again a little while, and you will see me;' and, 'Because I go to the Father?'" They said therefore, "What is this that he says, 'A little while?' We don't know what he is saying."

Therefore Jesus perceived that they wanted to ask him, and he said to them, **"Do you inquire among yourselves concerning this, that I said, 'A little while, and you won't see me, and again a little while, and you will see me?' Most assuredly I tell you, that you will weep and lament, but the world will rejoice. You will be sorrowful, but your sorrow will be turned into joy.**

"A woman, when she is in travail, has sorrow, because her time has come. But when she has delivered the child, she doesn't remember the anguish any more, for the joy that a child is born into the world. You therefore now have sorrow, but I will see you again, and your heart will rejoice, and no one will take your joy away from you.

"In that day you will ask me no question. Most assuredly I tell you, whatever you may ask of the Father in my name, he will give it to you. Until now, you have asked nothing in my name. Ask, and you will receive, that your joy may be made full.

Jesus has overcome the world

"I have spoken these things to you in figures of speech. But the time comes when I will no more speak to you in figures of speech, but will tell you plainly about the Father. In that day you will ask in my name; and I don't say to you, that I will pray to the Father for you, for the Father himself loves you, because you have loved me, and have believed that I came forth from God. I came out from the Father, and have come into the world. Again, I leave the world, and go to the Father."

His disciples said to him, "Behold, now you speak plainly, and speak no figures of speech. Now we know that you know all things, and don't need for anyone to question you. By this we believe that you came forth from God."

Jesus answered them, **"Do you now believe?** Behold, the time comes, yes, has now come, that you will be scattered, everyone to his own place, and will leave me alone. Yet I am not alone, because the Father is with me. I have told you these things, that in me you may have peace. In the world you have oppression; but cheer up! I have overcome the world."

Jesus prays for Himself

Source: Jn. 17:1-26

Jesus said these things, and lifting up his eyes to heaven, he said, "Father, the time has come. Glorify your Son, that your Son may also glorify you; even as you gave him authority over all flesh, that to all whom you have given him, he will give eternal life. This is eternal life, that they should know you, the only true God, and him whom you sent, Jesus Christ. I glorified you on the earth. I have accomplished the work which you have given me to do. Now, Father, glorify me with your own self with the glory which I had with you before the world existed.

Jesus prays for His disciples

"I revealed your name to the people whom you have given me out of the world. They were yours, and you have given them to me. They have kept your word. Now they know that all things whatever you have given me are from you, for the words which you have given me I have given to them, and they received them, and knew for sure that I came forth from you, and they believed that you sent me. I pray for them.

"I don't pray for the world, but for those whom you have given me, for they are yours. All things that are mine are yours, and yours are mine, and I am glorified in them. I am no more in the world, and these are in the world, and I am coming to you. Holy Father, keep them through your name which you have given me, that they may be one, even as we are. While I was with them in the world, I kept them in your name. Those whom you have given me I have kept. None of them is lost, except the son of perdition, that the Scripture might be fulfilled.

"But now I come to you, and I say these things in the world, that they may have my joy made full in themselves. I have given them your word. The world hated them, because they are not of the world, even as I am not of the world. I pray not that you would take them from the world, but that you would keep them from the evil one. They are not of the world even as I am not of the world. Sanctify them in your truth. Your word is truth. As you sent me into the world, even so I sent them into the world. For their sakes I sanctify myself, that they themselves also may be sanctified in truth.

Jesus prays for all believers
"Neither for these only do I pray, but for those also who believe in me through their word, that they may all be one; even as you, Father, are in me, and I in you, that they also may be one in us; that the world may believe that you sent me. The glory which you have given me, I have given to them; that they may be one, even as we are one; I in them, and you in me, that they may be perfected into one; that the world may know that you sent me, and loved them, even as you loved me.

"Father, I desire that they also whom you have given me be with me where I am, that they may see my glory, which you have given me, for you loved me before the foundation of the world. Righteous Father, the world didn't know you, but I knew you; and these knew that you sent me. I made known to them your name, and will make it known; that the love with which you loved me may be in them, and I in them."

[Jesus goes to the garden called Gethsemane, on the Mount of Olives, just east of Jerusalem]

Jesus prays in the garden

Location: Gethsemane
Source: Mt. 26:36 (+Lk. 22:40); Mk. 14:33; Mt. 26:37-38; Mk. 14:35-36; Lk. 22:42-44; Mk. 14:37; Mt. 26:40-46

Then Jesus came with them to a place called Gethsemane, and said to his disciples, **"Sit here, while I go there and pray. Pray that you don't enter into temptation."**

He took with him Peter, James, and John, and began to be sorrowful and severely troubled.

Then he said to them, **"My soul is exceedingly sorrowful, even to death. Stay here, and watch with me."**

He went forward a little, and fell on the ground, and prayed that, if it were possible, the hour might pass away from him.

He said, **"Abba, Father, all things are possible to you. Father, if you are willing, remove this cup from me. Nevertheless, not my will, but yours, be done."**

An angel from heaven appeared to him, strengthening him. Being in agony he prayed more earnestly. His sweat became like great drops of blood falling down on the ground.

He came and found them sleeping, and said to Peter, **"Simon, are you sleeping? Couldn't you watch with me for one hour? Watch and pray, that you don't enter into temptation. The spirit indeed is willing, but the flesh is weak."**

Again, a second time he went away, and prayed, saying, **"My Father, if this cup can't pass away from me, unless I drink it, your will be done."**

The Lord's Supper

He came again and found them sleeping, for their eyes were heavy.

He left them again, went away, and prayed a third time, saying the same words.

Then he came to his disciples, and said to them, **"Sleep on now, and take your rest. Behold, the hour is at hand, and the Son of Man is betrayed into the hands of sinners. Arise, let us be going. Behold, he who betrays me is at hand."**

— 23 —

Arrest and Trial

Judas completes his act of betrayal and Jesus is arrested. As Jesus predicted, Peter denies Him three times. Jesus goes through a series of trials or hearings, as one authority sends Him to another. There are three Jewish trials (before Annas, Caiaphas, and the Sanhedrin) and three Roman trials (before Pilot, Herod, and back to Pilot).

Betrayal and arrest in Gethsemane

Location: Gethsemane, Jerusalem   Source: Mt. 26:47-48; Lk. 22:47-48; Mt. 26:49-50; Jn. 18:4-9; Mt. 26:50; Lk. 22:49; Jn. 18:10-11; Mt. 26:52-54; Lk. 22:51; Mt. 26:55-56 (+Lk. 22:53)

While he was still speaking, behold, Judas, one of the twelve, came, and with him a great multitude with swords and clubs, from the chief priest and elders of the people. Now he who betrayed him gave them a sign, saying, "Whoever I will kiss, that is he. Take him." And he who was called Judas, one of the twelve, went in front of them. He came near to Jesus to kiss him.

But Jesus said to him, **"Judas, do you betray the Son of Man with a kiss?"**

Immediately he came to Jesus, and said, "Hail, Rabbi!" and kissed him.

Arrest and Trial

Jesus said to him, **"Friend, why are you here?"**

Jesus therefore, knowing all the things that were coming on him, went forth, and said to them, **"Who are you looking for?"**

They answered him, "Jesus of Nazareth."

Jesus said to them, **"I AM."**

Judas also, who betrayed him, was standing with them. When therefore he *[Jesus]* said to them, "I AM," they went backward, and fell to the ground.

Again therefore he asked them, **"Who are you looking for?"**

They said, "Jesus of Nazareth."

Jesus answered, **"I told you that I AM. If therefore you seek me, let these go their way,"** that the word might be fulfilled which he spoke, **"Of those whom you have given me, I have lost none."**

Then they came and laid hands on Jesus, and took him. When those who were around him saw what was about to happen, they said to him, "Lord, shall we strike with the sword?"

Simon Peter therefore, having a sword, drew it, and struck the high priest's servant, and cut off his right ear. The servant's name was Malchus.

Jesus therefore said to Peter, **"Put up the sword into its sheath. The cup which the Father has given me, shall I not drink it? Put your sword back into its place, for all those who take the sword will die by the sword. Or do you think that I can't ask my Father, and he** would even now send me more than twelve legions of angels? How then would the Scriptures be fulfilled that it must be so?"

But Jesus answered, "Let me at least do this" — and he touched his ear, and healed him.

In that hour Jesus said to the multitudes, "**Have you come out as against a robber with swords and clubs to seize me? I sat daily in the temple teaching, and you didn't arrest me. But this is your hour, and the power of darkness. But all this has happened, that the Scriptures of the prophets might be fulfilled.**"

Then all the disciples left him, and fled.

Jesus taken to Annas

Source: Jn. 18:12-14; Jn. 18:19-24

So the detachment, the commanding officer, and the officers of the Jews, seized Jesus and bound him, and led him to Annas first, for he was father-in-law to Caiaphas, who was high priest that year.[36] Now it was Caiaphas who gave counsel to the Jews, that it was expedient that one man should die for the people.

The high priest *[Annas]* therefore asked Jesus of his disciples, and of his teaching.

Jesus answered him, "**I spoke openly to the world. I always taught in synagogues, and in the temple, where the Jews always meet. I said nothing in secret. Why do you ask me? Ask those who have**

---

[36] Annas was the high priest from approximately 6 to 15 A.D. when the Romans removed him and subsequently appointed Caiaphas (the son-in-law of Annas) as high priest. Annas continued to be highly regarded by the Jews, continued to have significant influence, and the Jews continued to call him "high priest." But Caiaphas held the formal position and had the formal authority.

heard me what I said to them. Behold, these know the things which I said."

When he had said this, one of the officers standing by slapped Jesus with his hand, saying, "Do you answer the high priest like that?"

Jesus answered him, **"If I have spoken evil, testify of the evil; but if well, why do you beat me?"**

Annas sent him bound to Caiaphas, the high priest *[see footnote 36]*.

Peter denies Jesus three times
Source: Mk. 14:54, 66-72; Lk. 22:62

Peter had followed him afar off, until he came into the court of the high priest. He was sitting with the officers, and warming himself in the light of the fire.

As Peter was beneath in the court, one of the maids of the high priest came, and seeing Peter warming himself, she looked at him, and said, "You were also with the Nazarene, Jesus!"

But he denied it, saying, "I neither know, nor understand what you are saying." He went out into the porch, and the cock crowed.

The maid saw him, and began again to tell those who stood by, "This is one of them." But he again denied it.

After a little while again those who stood by said to Peter, "You truly are one of them, for you are a Galilean, and your speech shows it."

But he began to curse, and to swear, "I don't know this man of whom you speak!" The cock crowed the second time.

Peter remembered the word, how that Jesus said to him, "Before the cock crows twice, you will deny me three times."

When he thought about that, he went out, and wept bitterly.

Jesus faces Caiaphas and the Sanhedrin[37]
Source: Mt. 26:59-61; Mk. 14:58-60; Mt. 26:63-68

[After Jesus has been brought from Annas to Caiaphas.] Now the chief priests, the elders, and the whole council sought false testimony against Jesus, that they might put him to death; and they found none. Even though many false witnesses came forward, they found none. But at last two false witnesses came forward, and said, "We heard him say, 'I will destroy this temple that is made with hands, and in three days I will build another made without hands.'" Even so, their testimony did not agree.

The high priest stood up in the midst, and asked Jesus, "Have you no answer? What is it which these testify against you?"

But Jesus held his peace.

The high priest answered him, "I adjure you by the living God, that you tell us whether you are the Christ, the Son of God."

Jesus said to him, **"You have said it. Nevertheless, I tell you, henceforth you will see the Son of Man sitting at the right hand of Power, and coming on the clouds of the sky."**

Then the high priest tore his clothing, saying, "He has spoken blasphemy! Why do we need any more witnesses? Behold, now you have heard his blasphemy. What do you think?"

---

[37] The Sanhedrin was the supreme Jewish court of justice in Jerusalem.

Arrest and Trial

They answered, "He is worthy of death!"

Then they spit in his face and beat him with their fists, and some slapped him, saying, "Prophesy to us, you Christ! Who hit you?"

Jesus faces the Sanhedrin again at dawn (shortly after the above)
Source: Lk. 22:66-71

As soon as it was day, the assembly of the elders of the people was gathered together, both chief priests and scribes, and they led him away into their council, saying, "If you are the Christ, tell us."

But he said to them, **"If I tell you, you won't believe, and if I ask, you will in no way answer me or let me go. From now on, the Son of Man will be seated at the right hand of the power of God."**

They all said, "Are you then the Son of God?"

He said to them, **"You say it, because I AM."**

They said, "Why do we need any more witness? For we ourselves have heard from his own mouth!"

[Note: the remainder of this chapter contains very few words of Jesus, but the material quoted is essential to portray the events leading to his crucifixion and the suffering imposed on him.]

Jesus taken to Pilate[38]
Source: Mt. 27:1-2; Lk. 23:2-3; Mk. 15:3-5; Lk. 23:4-7

All the chief priests and the elders of the people took counsel against

---

[38] Pontius Pilate was the Roman governor of Judea. The Romans did not allow the Jews to impose capital punishment. Pilate would have to impose such punishment.

Jesus to put him to death: and they bound him, and led him away, and delivered him up to Pontius Pilate, the governor. They began to accuse him, saying, "We found this man perverting the nation, forbidding paying taxes to Caesar, and saying that he himself is Christ, a king."

Pilate asked him, "Are you the King of the Jews?"

He answered him, **"So you say."**

The chief priests accused him of many things. Pilate again asked him, "Have you no answer? See how many things they testify against you!"

But Jesus made no further answer, so Pilate marveled.

Pilate said to the chief priests and the multitudes, "I find no basis for a charge against this man." But they insisted, saying, "He stirs up the people, teaching throughout all Judea, beginning from Galilee even to this place."

But when Pilate heard Galilee mentioned, he asked if the man was a Galilean. When he found out that he was in Herod's jurisdiction, he sent him to Herod[39], who was also in Jerusalem in those days.

Jesus faces Herod

Source: Lk. 23:8-12

Now when Herod saw Jesus, he was exceedingly glad, for he had wanted to see him for a long time, because he had heard many things about him. He hoped to see some miracle done by him. He questioned him with many words, but he gave no answers. The chief priests and the scribes stood, vehemently accusing him. Herod with his soldiers humiliated him and mocked him. Dressing him in luxurious clothing,

---

[39] Herod was the Roman governor who had responsibility for Galilee.

they sent him back to Pilate. Herod and Pilate became friends with each other that very day, for before that they were enemies with each other.

Jesus faces Pilate for the second time
Barabbas released
Source: Lk. 23:13-15; Mt. 27:15-18; Mt. 27:21-24;
Lk. 23:24; Mt. 27:26-30; Jn. 19:4-16; Mt. 27:31

Pilate called together the chief priests and the rulers and the people, and said to them, "You brought this man to me as one that perverts the people, and see, I have examined him before you, and found no basis for a charge against this man concerning those things of which you accuse him. Neither has Herod, for I sent you to him, and see, nothing worthy of death has been done by him.

Now at the feast the governor used to release to the multitude one prisoner, whom they wanted. They had then a notable prisoner, called Barabbas. When therefore they were gathered together, Pilate said to them, "Whom do you want me to release to you? Barabbas, or Jesus, who is called Christ?" For he knew that because of envy they had delivered him up.

They said, "Barabbas!"

Pilate said to them, "What then will I do to Jesus, who is called Christ?"

They all said to him, "Let him be crucified!"

But the governor said, "Why? What evil has he done?"

But they cried out exceedingly, saying, "Let him be crucified!"

So when Pilate saw that nothing was gained, but rather that a disturbance was starting, he took water, and washed his hands before the multitude, saying, "I am innocent of the blood of this righteous person. You see to it."

Pilate adjudged that what they asked for should be done. Then he released to them Barabbas, but Jesus he flogged and delivered to be crucified.

Then the governor's soldiers took Jesus into the Praetorium, and gathered to him the whole cohort. They stripped him, and put a scarlet robe on him. They braided a crown of thorns and put it on his head, and a reed in his right hand; and they kneeled down before him, and mocked him, saying, "Hail, King of the Jews!" They spat on him, and took the reed and struck him on the head.

Then Pilate went out again, and said to them, "Behold, I bring him out to you, that you may know that I find no basis for a charge against him."

Jesus therefore came out, wearing the crown of thorns and the purple garment. Pilate said to them, "Behold, the man!"

When therefore the chief priests and the officers saw him, they cried out, saying, "Crucify! Crucify!"

Pilate said to them, "Take him yourselves, and crucify him, for I find no basis for a charge against him."

The Jews answered him, "We have a law, and by our law he ought to die, because he made himself the Son of God."

When therefore Pilate heard this saying, he was more afraid. He en-

Arrest and Trial

tered into the Praetorium again, and said to Jesus, "Where are you from?"

But Jesus gave him no answer.

Pilate therefore said to him, "Aren't you speaking to me? Don't you know that I have power to release you, and have power to crucify you?"

Jesus answered, **"You would have no power at all against me, unless it were given to you from above. Therefore he who delivered me to you has greater sin."**

At this, Pilate sought to release him, but the Jews cried out, saying, "If you release this man, you aren't Caesar's friend! Everyone who makes himself a king speaks against Caesar!"

When Pilate therefore heard these words, he brought Jesus out, and sat down on the judgment seat at a place called "The Pavement," but in Hebrew, "Gabbatha." Now it was the Preparation of the Passover. He said to the Jews, "Behold, your King!"

They cried out, "Away with him! Away with him! Crucify him!"

Pilate said to them, "Shall I crucify your King?"

The chief priests answered, "We have no king but Caesar!"

Then therefore he delivered him to them to be crucified. So they took the robe off from him, and put his clothes on him, and led him away to crucify him.

— 24 —

Crucifixion, Death, Burial

Jesus undergoes crucifixion, a particularly cruel and tortuous death. He is taken from the cross and buried. In this sacrifice of His earthly life, He takes on the sin of all humanity, which opens a new covenant between God and man.

Jesus taken to Golgotha to be crucified[40]

Location: just outside Jerusalem Source: Jn. 19:17; Lk. 23:26-32; Mk. 15:22-23

He went out, bearing his cross. When they led him away, they grabbed one Simon of Cyrene, coming from the country, and laid on him the cross, to carry it after Jesus. A great multitude of the people followed him, including women who also mourned and lamented him.

But Jesus, turning to them, said, **"Daughters of Jerusalem, don't weep for me, but weep for yourselves and for your children. For behold, the days are coming in which they will say, 'Blessed are the barren, the wombs that never bore, and the breasts that never nursed.' Then will they begin to tell the mountains, 'Fall on us!' and to the hills, 'Cover us.' For if they do these things in the green tree, what will be done in the dry?"**

There were also others, two criminals, led with him to be put to death. They brought him to the place called Golgotha, which is, being

---

[40] A hill near the city wall

Crucifixion, Death, Burial

interpreted, "The place of a skull." They offered him wine mixed with myrrh to drink,[41] but he didn't take it.

On the Cross
Source: Mk. 15:25, 27-28; Jn. 19:19-22; Lk. 23:34; Jn. 19:23-27; Lk. 23:39-43

It was the third hour *[9 am]*, and they crucified him.

With him they crucified two robbers; one on his right hand, and one on his left. The Scripture was fulfilled, which says, "He was numbered with transgressors.[42]"

Pilate wrote a title also, and put it on the cross. There was written, "JESUS OF NAZARETH, THE KING OF THE JEWS." Therefore many of the Jews read this title, for the place where Jesus was crucified was near the city; and it was written in Hebrew, in Latin, and in Greek. The chief priests of the Jews therefore said to Pilate, "Don't write, 'The King of the Jews,' but that, 'he said, I am King of the Jews.'"

Pilate answered, "What I have written, I have written."

Jesus said, **"Father, forgive them, for they don't know what they are doing."**

Then the soldiers, when they had crucified Jesus, took his garments and made four parts, to every soldier a part; and also the coat. Now the coat was without seam, woven from the top throughout. Then they said to one another, "Let's not tear it, but cast lots for it, whose it will be," that the Scripture might be fulfilled, which says,

---

[41] Offered to dull pain. Jesus chose to fully suffer the pain.

[42] Isaiah 53:12

> "They parted my garments among them.
> For my cloak they cast lots."[43]

Therefore the soldiers did these things.

But there were standing by the cross of Jesus his mother, and his mother's sister, Mary the wife of Clopas, and Mary Magdalene.

Therefore when Jesus saw his mother, and the disciple whom he loved[44] standing there, he said to his mother, **"Woman, behold your son!"** Then he said to the disciple, **"Behold, your mother!"**

From that hour, the disciple took her to his own home.

One of the criminals who was hanged insulted him, saying, "If you are the Christ, save yourself and us!" But the other answered, and rebuking him said, "Don't you even fear God, seeing you are in the same condemnation? And we indeed justly, for we receive the due reward for our deeds, but this man has done nothing wrong." He said to Jesus, "Lord, remember me when you come into your kingdom."

Jesus said to him, **"Assuredly I tell you, today you will be with me in Paradise."**

Jesus dies on the cross
Source: Lk. 23:44; Mk. 15:34; Jn. 19:28-30; Lk. 23:46; Mt. 27:51-54; Lk. 23:48; Mt. 27:55-56; Jn. 19:31-37

It was now about the sixth hour *[12 noon]*, and darkness came over the whole land until the ninth hour *[3 pm]*.

---

[43] Psalm 22:18

[44] This is John, the author of the Gospel of John. He refers to himself as "the disciple whom Jesus loved" several times in his Gospel.

Crucifixion, Death, Burial

At the ninth hour Jesus cried with a loud voice, saying, **"Eloi, Eloi, lama sabachthani?"** which is, being interpreted, **"My God, my God, why have you forsaken me?"**

After this, Jesus, seeing that all things were now finished, that the Scripture might be fulfilled, said, **"I am thirsty."**

Now a vessel full of vinegar was set there; so they put a sponge full of the vinegar on hyssop, and brought it to his mouth.

When Jesus therefore had received the vinegar, he said, **"It is finished."** Jesus, crying with a loud voice, said, **"Father, into your hands I commit my spirit!"**

Having said this, he breathed his last.

Behold, the veil of the temple was torn in two from the top to the bottom.[45] The earth quaked and the rocks were split. The tombs were opened, and many bodies of the saints who had fallen asleep were raised; and coming forth out of the tombs after his resurrection, they entered into the holy city and appeared to many.

Now the centurion, and those who were with him watching Jesus, when they saw the earthquake, and the things that were done, feared exceedingly, saying, "Truly this was the Son of God."

All the multitudes that came together to see this, when they saw the things that were done, returned beating their breasts. Many women were there watching from afar, who had followed Jesus from Galilee, serving him, among whom was Mary Magdalene, Mary the mother of James and Joses, and *[Salome]* the mother of the sons of Zebedee.

---

[45] This is highly symbolic. The veil of the temple separated all but the high priest from the presence of God in the inner chamber, the "holy of holies." Hereafter, all have direct access to God through Jesus Christ.

Therefore the Jews, because it was the Preparation, so that the bodies wouldn't remain on the cross on the Sabbath (for that Sabbath was a special one), asked of Pilate that their legs might be broken,[46] and that they might be taken away.

Therefore the soldiers came, and broke the legs of the first, and of the other who was crucified with him; but when they came to Jesus, and saw that he was already dead, they didn't break his legs. However one of the soldiers pierced his side with a spear, and immediately blood and water came out.

He who has seen has testified, and his testimony is true. He knows that he tells the truth, that you may believe. For these things happened, that the Scripture might be fulfilled, "A bone of him will not be broken."[47] Again another Scripture says, "They will look on him whom they pierced."[48]

Jesus is buried in Joseph's tomb
Source: Mk. 15:42-45 (+Jn. 19:38); Jn. 19:39-40; Mt. 27:59-66

When evening had now come, because it was the Preparation, that is, the day before the Sabbath, Joseph of Arimathaea, a member of the council of honorable estate, who also himself was looking for the kingdom of God, being a disciple of Jesus, but secretly for fear of the Jews, boldly went in to Pilate, and asked for Jesus' body.

Pilate marveled if he were already dead: and calling to him the centurion, he asked him whether he had been dead for a while. When he learned it from the centurion, he granted the body to Joseph.

---

[46] So that they could not support themselves and would die sooner, before the Sabbath.
[47] Exodus 12:46, Numbers 9:12, Psalm 34:20
[48] Zechariah 12:10

Crucifixion, Death, Burial

Nicodemus also came, he who at first came to Jesus by night, bringing a mixture of myrrh and aloes, about a hundred Roman pounds. So they took Jesus' body, and bound it in linen cloths with the spices, as the custom of the Jews is to bury.

Joseph took the body, and wrapped it in a clean linen cloth, and laid it in his own new tomb, which he had hewn out in the rock, and he rolled a great stone to the door of the tomb, and departed. Mary Magdalene was there, and the other Mary, sitting opposite the tomb.

Now on the next day, which is the day after the Preparation, the chief priests and the Pharisees were gathered together to Pilate, saying, "Sir, we remember what that deceiver said while he was still alive: 'After three days I will rise again.' Command therefore that the tomb be made secure until the third day, lest perhaps his disciples come at night and steal him away, and tell the people, 'He is risen from the dead;' and the last deception will be worse than the first."

Pilate said to them, "You have a guard. Go, make it as secure as you can."

So they went, and made the tomb secure, sealing the stone, the guard being with them.

— 25 —

Resurrection!

This chapter relates the foundational event of Christianity, celebrated by Christians on Easter: the resurrection of Jesus after His death on the cross. As summarized in 1Timothy 2:5,6, " For there is one God, and one mediator between God and men, the man Christ Jesus, who gave himself as a ransom for all." This chapter also includes the moving words of the disciple Thomas when he finally believes Jesus has risen: "my Lord, and my God."

The empty tomb

Location: the tomb; Jerusalem					Source: Mt. 28:2-4; Mk. 16:1-8

Behold, there was a great earthquake, for an angel of the Lord descended from the sky, and came and rolled away the stone from the door, and sat on it. His appearance was like lightning, and his clothing white as snow. For fear of him, the guards shook, and became like dead men.

When the Sabbath *[Saturday]* was past, Mary Magdalene, and Mary the mother of James, and Salome, bought spices, that they might come and anoint him. Very early on the first day of the week *[Sunday]*, they came to the tomb when the sun had risen. They were saying among themselves, "Who will roll away the stone from the door of the tomb for us?" for it was very big. Looking up, they saw that the stone was rolled back.

Resurrection!

Entering into the tomb, they saw a young man sitting on the right side, dressed in a white robe, and they were amazed. He said to them, "Don't be amazed. You seek Jesus, the Nazarene, who has been crucified. He has risen. He is not here. Behold, the place where they laid him! But go, tell his disciples and Peter, 'He goes before you into Galilee. There you will see him, as he said to you.'"

They went out, and fled from the tomb

[Mary Magdalene runs ahead and tells the disciples. Peter and John visit the tomb and find it empty. Apparently Mary returned with them.]

Jesus appears to Mary Magdalene
Source: Jn. 20:11,14-18

Mary was standing outside at the tomb weeping. She turned herself back, and saw Jesus standing, and didn't know that it was Jesus.

Jesus said to her, **"Woman, why are you weeping? Who are you looking for?"**

She, supposing him to be the gardener, said to him, "Sir, if you have carried him away, tell me where you have laid him, and I will take him away."

Jesus said to her, **"Mary."**

She turned herself, and said to him, "Rhabbouni!" which is to say, "Teacher!"

Jesus said to her, **"Don't touch me, for I haven't yet ascended to my Father; but go to my brothers, and tell them, 'I am ascending to my Father and your Father, and my God and your God.'"**

Mary Magdalene came and told the disciples that she had seen the Lord, and that he had said these things to her.

Jesus appears to the other women
Location: Near JerusalemSource: Mt. 28:9-10

As they *[the other women]* went to tell his disciples, behold, Jesus met them, saying, **"Rejoice!"**

They came and took hold of his feet, and worshiped him.

Then Jesus said to them, **"Don't be afraid. Go tell my brothers that they may go into Galilee, and there they will see me."**

The soldiers report to the chief priests, and are bribed
Location: JerusalemSource: Mt. 28:11-15

Now while they were going, behold, some of the guards came into the city, and told the chief priests all the things that had happened. When they were assembled with the elders, and had taken counsel, they gave a large amount of silver to the soldiers, saying, "Say that his disciples came by night, and stole him away while we slept. If this comes to the governor's ears, we will persuade him and make you free of worry."[49] So they took the money and did as they were told. This saying was spread abroad among the Jews, and continues until this day.

Jesus appears to two disciples on the road to Emmaus
Location: Near JerusalemSource: Lk. 24:13-27

Behold, two of them were going that very day to a village named Emmaus, which was sixty stadia from Jerusalem. They talked with each other about all of these things which had happened. It happened, while they talked and questioned together, that Jesus himself came

---

[49] A soldier could be put to death for falling asleep on guard duty.

Resurrection!

near, and went with them. But their eyes were kept from recognizing him.

He said to them, **"What are you talking about as you walk, and are sad?"**

One of them, named Cleopas, answered him, "Are you the only stranger in Jerusalem who doesn't know the things which have happened there in these days?"

He said to them, **"What things?"**

They said to him, "The things concerning Jesus, the Nazarene, who was a prophet mighty in deed and word before God and all the people; and how the chief priests and our rulers delivered him up to be condemned to death, and crucified him. But we were hoping that it was he who would redeem Israel. Yes, and besides all this, it is now the third day since these things happened. Also, certain women of our company amazed us, having arrived early at the tomb; and when they didn't find his body, they came saying that they had also seen a vision of angels, who said that he was alive. Some of us went to the tomb, and found it just like the women had said, but they didn't see him."

He said to them, **"Foolish men, and slow of heart to believe in all that the prophets have spoken! Didn't the Christ have to suffer these things, and to enter into his glory?"**

Beginning from Moses and from all the prophets, he explained to them in all the Scriptures the things concerning himself.

Jesus appears to disciples (without Thomas)

Location: Jerusalem
Source: Jn. 20:19; Lk. 24:37-40; Jn. 20:20-23; Lk. 24:41-43

When therefore it was evening, on that day, the first day of the week, and when the doors were locked where the disciples were assembled, for fear of the Jews, Jesus came and stood in the midst, and said to them, **"Peace be to you."**

But they were terrified and filled with fear, and supposed that they saw a spirit.

He said to them, **"Why are you troubled? Why do doubts arise in your hearts? See my hands and my feet, that it is truly me. Touch me and see, for a spirit doesn't have flesh and bones, as you see that I have."**

When he had said this, he shown them his hands and his feet. He showed them his hands and his side. The disciples therefore were glad when they saw the Lord.

Jesus therefore said to them again, **"Peace be to you. As the Father has sent me, even so I send you."**

When he had said this, he breathed on them, and said to them, **"Receive the Holy Spirit! Whoever's sins you forgive, they are forgiven to them. Whoever's sins you retain, they are retained."**

While they still didn't believe for joy, and wondered, he said to them, **"Do you have anything here to eat?"**

They gave him a piece of a broiled fish and some honeycomb. He took it, and ate in front of them.

Resurrection!

Thomas sees and believes

Source: Jn. 20:24-29

But Thomas, one of the twelve, called Didymus *[the twin]*, wasn't with them when Jesus came. The other disciples therefore said to him, "We have seen the Lord!" But he said to them, "Unless I see in his hands the print of the nails, and put my hand into his side, I will not believe."

After eight days again his disciples were within, and Thomas with them. Jesus came, the doors being locked, and stood in the midst, and said, **"Peace be to you."**

Then he said to Thomas, **"Reach here your finger, and see my hands. Reach here your hand, and put it into my side. Don't be faithless, but believing."**

Thomas answered him, "My Lord and my God!"

Jesus said to him, **"Because you have seen me, you have believed. Blessed are those who have not seen, and have believed."**

Jesus appears to disciples at the sea

Location: Sea of Galilee *Source: Jn. 21:1-23*

After these things, Jesus revealed himself again to the disciples at the sea of Tiberias *[Sea of Galilee]*. He revealed himself this way. Simon Peter, Thomas called Didymus, Nathanael of Cana in Galilee, and the sons of Zebedee, and two others of his disciples were together. Simon Peter said to them, "I'm going fishing." They told him, "We are also coming with you." They immediately went forth, and entered into the boat. That night, they caught nothing.

But when day was now breaking, Jesus stood on the beach, yet the disciples didn't know that it was Jesus.

Jesus therefore said to them, **"Children, have you anything to eat?"**

They answered him, "No."

He said to them, **"Cast the net on the right side of the boat, and you will find some."**

They cast therefore, and now they were not able to draw it in for the multitude of fish.

That disciple therefore whom Jesus loved *[John]* said to Peter, "It's the Lord!"

So when Simon Peter heard that it was the Lord, he wrapped his coat around him (for he was naked), and threw himself into the sea. But the other disciples came in the little boat (for they were not far from the land, but about two hundred cubits away), dragging the net full of fish. So when they got out on the land, they saw a fire of coals there, and fish laid on it, and bread.

Jesus said to them, **"Bring some of the fish which you have just caught."**

Simon Peter went up, and drew the net to land, full of great fish, one hundred fifty-three; and even though there were so many, the net wasn't torn.

Jesus said to them, **"Come and eat breakfast."**

None of the disciples dared inquire of him, "Who are you?" knowing that it was the Lord. Then Jesus came and took the bread, gave it to them, and the fish likewise.

Resurrection!

This is now the third time that Jesus was revealed to his disciples, after he had risen from the dead.

Jesus questions Peter three times
So when they had eaten their breakfast, Jesus said to Simon Peter, **"Simon, son of Jonah, do you love me more than these?"**

He said to him, "Yes, Lord; you know that I have affection for you."

He said to him, **"Feed my lambs."**

He said to him again a second time, **"Simon, son of Jonah, do you love me?"**

He said to him, "Yes, Lord; you know that I have affection for you."

He said to him, **"Tend my sheep."**

He said to him the third time, **"Simon, son of Jonah, do you have affection for me?"**

Peter was grieved because he asked him the third time, "Do you have affection for me?" He said to him, "Lord, you know everything. You know that I have affection for you."

Jesus said to him, **"Feed my sheep. Most assuredly I tell you, when you were young, you dressed yourself, and walked where you wanted to. But when you are old, you will stretch out your hands, and another will dress you, and carry you where you don't want to go."**

Now he said this, signifying by what kind of death he would glorify God. When he had said this, he said to him, **"Follow me."**

Then Peter, turning around, saw a disciple following. This was the disciple whom Jesus sincerely loved *[John]*, the one who had also leaned on Jesus' breast at the supper and asked, "Lord, who is going to betray You?" Peter seeing him, said to Jesus, "Lord, and what will this man do?"

Jesus said to him, **"If I desire that he stay until I come, what is that to you? You follow me."**

This saying therefore went forth among the brothers, that this disciple wouldn't die. Yet Jesus didn't say to him that he wouldn't die, but, "If I desire that he stay until I come, what is that to you?"

— 26 —

Great Commission

After His resurrection, Jesus continues appearing to numerous persons over many weeks. During this time He gives the "great commission" to spread the Gospel to the World (not just to the Jews). He also promises the support and help of the Holy Spirit.

The "Great Commission" to spread the Gospel to the world

Location: A mountain in Galilee Source: Mt. 28:16; Lk. 24:44-49; Mk. 16:15-18; Mt. 28:18-20

The eleven disciples went into Galilee, to the mountain where Jesus had sent them.

He said to them, **"This is what I told you, while I was still with you, that all things which are written in the law of Moses, the prophets, and the psalms, concerning me must be fulfilled."**

Then he opened their minds, that they might understand the Scriptures.

He said to them, **"Thus it is written, and thus it was necessary for the Christ to suffer and to rise from the dead the third day, and that repentance and remission of sins should be preached in his name to all the nations, beginning at Jerusalem. You are witnesses of these things. Behold, I send forth the promise of my Father on you. But wait in the city of Jerusalem until you are clothed with power from on high."**

He said to them, "Go into all the world, and preach the gospel to the whole creation. He who believes and is baptized will be saved; but he who disbelieves will be condemned. These signs will accompany those who believe: in my name they will cast out demons; they will speak with new languages; they will take up serpents, and if they drink any deadly thing, it will in no way hurt them; they will lay hands on the sick, and they will recover."

Jesus came to them and spoke to them, saying, "All authority has been given to me in heaven and on earth. Go, and make disciples of all nations, baptizing them in the name of the Father and of the Son and of the Holy Spirit, teaching them to observe all things which I commanded you. Behold, I am with you always, even to the end of the age."

[Over a period of 40 days after His resurrection, Jesus appeared numerous times to various people and groups. The following is the last such time recorded.]

The Holy Spirit promised by Jesus
Location: Jerusalem Source: Acts 1:4-8

Being assembled together with them, he charged them, "Don't depart from Jerusalem, but wait for the promise of the Father, which you heard from me. For John indeed baptized in water, but you will be baptized in the Holy Spirit not many days from now."

Therefore, when they had come together, they asked him, "Lord, are you now restoring the kingdom to Israel?"

He said to them, "It isn't for you to know times or seasons which the Father has set within His own authority. But you will receive power when the Holy Spirit has come on you. You will be witnesses to me in Jerusalem, in all Judea and Samaria, and to the uttermost parts of the earth."

Great Commission

The Ascension—Jesus received into heaven

Location: Bethany Source: Lk. 24:50; Acts 1:9-11

He led them out as far as to Bethany, and he lifted up his hands, and blessed them. As they were looking, he was taken up, and a cloud received him out of their sight. While they were looking steadfastly into the sky as he went, behold, two men stood by them in white clothing, who also said, "You men of Galilee, why do you stand looking into the sky? This Jesus, who was received up from you into the sky will come back in the same way as you saw him going into the sky."

John's testimony at the end of his Gospel

Source: Jn. 20:30-31; Jn. 21:25

Jesus did many other signs in the presence of his disciples, which are not written in this book; but these are written, that you may believe that Jesus is the Christ, the Son of God, and that believing you may have life in his name.

There are also many other things which Jesus did, which if they would all be written, I suppose that even the world itself wouldn't contain the books that would be written.

APPENDIX

A. Methodology

I think it necessary to document the criteria I used and the general judgments I made in putting this book together.

1. General Approach

The intent is simple: take what Jesus said as recorded in the four Gospels (and that little bit at the first of Acts) and put it all together in chronological order with enough surrounding biblical text to provide context (with the words of Jesus in **bold**).

But in practice, there were complexities. Before describing those, let me summarize my basic approach:

1. I follow the chronology provided in documents typically entitled a "Harmony of the Gospels." These may be found in many study Bibles and on the Internet. They take all events found in all four Gospels, list them in probable chronological order, and show which verses in each Gospel refer to each event. It is not possible to be 100% sure of chronological order in all cases, so a few conflicts exist among various versions of Harmonies of the Gospels (more about that below).

   I am, of course, selecting the subset of events that involve the words of Jesus. Some events are described in only one Gospel, some in two or three Gospels, and some are described in all four Gospels.

2. When only one Gospel describes an event, that is the Gospel account I use (the easy case!).

3. When more than one Gospel describes the same event, I use just

one of those Gospel accounts if it is complete, meaning it includes all the content of the other Gospel accounts (the emphasis being on "content" even if a few words are different).

My next choice is to start with the one having the most detail and insert additional detail (verses or partial verses) from other Gospels. In a few cases, this leads to a significant amount of "cut and paste" among multiple gospel accounts (that can get a bit complicated).

In putting things together, I have almost always been able to use complete verses rather than partial verses, but there are exceptions. Of course, the division of the Bible into chapter and verse is not a part of the original biblical text anyway, so using partial verses isn't undesirable. Just realize that a verse listing in my source documentation could mean only part of the verse was used.

The source and order of all verses used in this book is documented as described in the following Section, "Notation."

4. I have adopted the guideline that moderately differing versions of the same event in multiple Gospels are all accurate, describing differing sub-events or additional aspects.

As noted in the Introduction, the intent and emphasis is on what Jesus actually said (rendered in **bold**) and did. But a significant amount of surrounding biblical text is included to place His words or actions in context or to describe major events affecting His actions. In a few cases, this results in extended passages without His words. (These occur mainly around his arrest, trial, crucifixion, and resurrection.)

2. More Detail

The above gives the basic approach. This section provides more detail and addresses several special situations. I think it necessary to document this additional detail, but realize most readers will have no interest and may choose to ignore the rest of this section. That's quite okay!

The problem is that the gospel writers did not always maintain chronological order within their own gospel. And each writer included only the events (or part of events) chosen for their purpose and audience. Because each gospel writer had a different audience and different intent, each produced different content.

The general chronology of events in all four gospels has been studied, debated, and documented by biblical scholars for many decades, resulting in a "Harmony of the Gospels" as mentioned above. But there is insufficient data in the gospels to be totally sure of chronology in all cases. Correct order is sometimes clear, sometimes is inferred with relatively high confidence, but in a few cases, is an educated guess. For this reason, different versions of the Harmonies of the Gospels exist. They largely agree, but some differences exist among versions. So we are left with residual uncertainty in some cases as to exact chronological order.

In writing this book, I consulted a number of Harmony of the Gospels versions and generally followed consensus where conflicts existed. These cases are usually quite minor.

However, the original gospel authors (inspired by God) were not so concerned with chronological exactness, so you and I shouldn't be either. Bottom line: the chronology followed in this book is generally correct, but no one can guarantee it is exactly correct.

There are four specific uncertainties worth highlighting:

1. Matthew 12:22-45 and Luke 11:14-32 contain nearly identical events and wording. Nevertheless, of the many versions of Harmonies of the Gospels I consulted, only one treats these as the same occasion. The others place the events in Luke well after the events in Matthew. I have done likewise, the two occasions being presented in chapters 5 and 12 of this book.

There are many examples in the Gospels where Jesus clearly repeated the same parable or comment more than once or was presented with the same situation more than once (I note a number of these in footnotes). So it's plausible to assume the above is one more such case, even if a fairly major one.

2. Each gospel describes one incident of Jesus being anointed with oil. Luke describes anointing of Jesus' feet with ointment (or fragrant oil) by "a woman ...who was a sinner." John describes the anointing of Jesus' feet with nard (or oil of spikenard) by Mary, the sister of Lazarus. Matthew and Mark describe the anointing of Jesus' head with an alabaster jar of ointment (or oil of spikenard) by "a woman." There is a large amount of similar detail in all four accounts, but differences also.

Scholars have debated whether all these are the same incident or multiple incidents. The discussion can get quite technical and detailed and has engendered a large body of analysis with differing expert opinion, all well beyond the scope of this Appendix.

Most everyone agrees Luke's account is a separate incident from the other three and occurs far earlier in the chronology. And most agree that Matthew and Mark are describing the same incident. So that leaves the question of whether John is describing the same incident as

Matthew/Mark. There are decent arguments both ways. Skipping a long (!) story, I'm following those who believe John, Matthew, and Mark are all describing the same incident. So for this compilation of *What Did Jesus Say?* I have two anointing incidents: Luke's and the one reported by Matthew, Mark, and John.

3. This regards the order of events during the Passover meal in the upper room in which Jesus institutes the Lord's Supper. Describing this evening, Matthew, Mark, and John have no conflict among themselves in the order of events as presented in their gospels. But Luke has a different ordering in a few cases. The gospel writers did not always report in chronological order, and many think Luke was describing things in a topical order. I follow the ordering given in Matthew, Mark, and John.

4. In the upper room on the night of Passover and the Lord's Supper, Simon Peter swears he will go with Christ to death if need be, that he will not deny him. Jesus replies that Peter will deny him three times that very night before the rooster crows. This event is reported in all four Gospels. One viewpoint (perhaps the correct one!) is that all are reporting the same one-time exchange. That is, Peter declares his intent once, and Jesus answers once.

However, the wording in three of the four Gospel accounts is sufficiently different that it is difficult (for me) to see how they could really be the exact same one-time exchange without one or two of the gospel accounts being technically inaccurate, even if in a minor way. I could not combine them into a one-time exchange without omitting (in my view) significant biblical text.

I struggled with that. I ended up using three gospel accounts. In my assimilation, Peter and Jesus have three sequential exchanges on this topic, as might well happen in such a conversation. And these three sequential exchanges also form a strikingly parallel (to me) to the three times Peter will deny Christ that night. (Interestingly, there are also two other cases of "triples" involving Jesus and Peter: Peter is found asleep three times in the Garden before Jesus is arrested, and Jesus asks Peter three times if he loves Him when He appears after His crucifixion.)

In conclusion, I risk getting you (the reader) too concerned about such technical detail. To the general reader, none of the above should matter much, if at all. I am only combining and assimilating existing biblical text. The issue is how well this has been done. But in any case, these are still the words of Jesus and surrounding events as reported in the four Gospels and that bit of Acts. And that's the main intent.

B. Notation

In Chapters 1-26 I've used the following format:

Except for chapter titles, footnotes, and text in italics, all text is directly from the *World English Bible* translation. The words of Jesus are in **bold** to distinguish them from surrounding biblical text.

Except for chapter titles and footnotes, italics are used to designate non-biblical text such as subheadings, explanatory notes, or comments.

Beneath each subheading, and to the left, is the physical location of all or most of events in the biblical text that follows. If no location is given, it remains the same as the previous indication.

Beneath each subheading, and to the right, are biblical references to the material assembled thereafter. Again, if none is given, it is a continuation of the previous indication. This is only for documentation purposes, and most readers can simply ignore it. I use two-letter designations for the Gospels:

    Mt. = Matthew
    Mk. = Mark
    Lk. = Luke
    Jn. = John

Other than that, I follow traditional practice. So "Mt. 8:3-5" means Matthew, chapter 8, verses 3-5. In a few cases, only part of the verse is used.

In very rare cases, I've added a few words from one verse within a sequence of other verses. I've indicated this by the following notation: Lk. 7:4-9 (+Mt. 8:5), meaning that a word or words from Matthew, chapter 8, verse 5, has been inserted within verses 4-9 of Luke, chapter 7. Again, I've done this in only a very few cases.

About the Author

RALPH WILLIAMS is a Ph.D. in physics, now retired, who spent his career in the semiconductor industry. He has been a committed Christian since childhood and has nursed the concept of this book for over a decade. He believes this book's approach is unique, focusing on the total words of Jesus, and will inspire others as it has him. Ralph and his wife live in a suburb of Dallas, TX.

To contact the author, e-mail him at ralphwilliamsmail@gmail.com

www.ingramcontent.com/pod-product-compliance
Lightning Source LLC
Chambersburg PA
CBHW050315120526
44592CB00014B/1912